<u>Biography</u>

James Egan was born in 1985 and grew up in
Portarlington, Co. Laois in the Midlands of Ireland.
In 2008, James moved to England and studied in Oxford.
James married his wife in 2012 and currently lives in
Havant in Hampshire.
James had his first book, 365 Ways to Stop Sabotaging
Your Life, published in 2014.
Several of James' books have become No.1 Best Sellers
in the UK including 1000 Facts about Horror Movies,
3000 Facts About the Greatest Movies Ever, 365 Things
People Believe That Aren't True, Another 365 Things
People Believe That Aren't True, and 500 Things People
Believe That Aren't True.

Books by James Egan

Fairytale
Inherit the Earth
Inherit the Earth: The Animal Kingdom
1000 Facts About the United States
Words That Need to Exist in English
Hilarious Things That Kids Say
Hilarious Things That Mums Say
1000 Facts about TV Shows Vol. 1-3
1000 Facts about Animated Shows Vol. 1-3
1000 Facts about Actors Vol. 1-3
1000 Facts about Countries Vol. 1-3
Dinosaurs Had Feathers (and other Random Facts)
1000 Facts about Animals Vol. 1-3
1000 Facts about James Bond
1000 Inspiring Facts
How to Psychologically Survive Cancer
1000 Out-of-this-World Facts about Space
1000 Facts about the Greatest Movies Ever Vol. 1-3
1000 Facts about Film Directors
1000 Facts about Superhero Movies Vol. 1-3
1000 Facts about Superheroes Vol. 1-3
1000 Facts about Supervillains Vol. 1-3
1000 Facts about Comic Books Vol. 1-3
1000 Facts about Animated Films Vol. 1-3
1000 Facts about Horror Movies Vol. 1-3
1000 Facts about American Presidents
Adorable Animal Facts
1000 Facts about Video Games Vol. 1-3
Things People Believe That Aren't True Vol. 1-4
1000 Fact about Film Director
The Mega Misconception Book
3000 Astounding Quotes
1000 Facts About Comic Book Characters Vol. 1-3
100 Classic Stories in 100 Pages
500 Facts about Godzilla
365 Ways to Stop Sabotaging Your Life
Flat Earthers Around the Globe
1000 Facts about Historic Figures Vol. 1-3
1000 Facts About Writers
1000 Facts about Ireland
The Biggest Movie Plotholes
1000 Facts about the Human Body

3000 Facts About Animated Films

By

James Egan

ISBN: 978-0244023362

Lulu Publishing Services rev. date: 01/09/2017

Contents

101 Dalmatians
1961

1. 101 Dalmatians cost $4 million. If this film didn't do well, Disney would've shut down its animation studio. 101 Dalmatians grossed $215 million, making it the most successful animated film ever in its time.

2. Only six puppies are named – Patch, Penny, Pepper, Freckles, Lucky, and Rolly.

3. The story was written by Dodie Smith. Her Dalmatians had 15 puppies as is depicted in the film.

4. Betty Loud Gerson voices Cruella De Vil and Miss Birdwell. She was also the Narrator for the animated film, Cinderella.

5. Every animated Disney musical has at least three songs except for this one, which only has two.

6. Clarence Nash provided the barks for the Dalmatians. He is most famous for providing the voice of Donald Duck.

7. The dogs from Lady and the Tramp make a cameo.

8. Walt Disney was so unhappy with the animation that he never forgave the animator until his dying day.

9. The film spawned an animated series in 1997. It was cancelled after one season.

10.   The live-action remake of 101 Dalmatians was released in 1996. 230 Dalmatian puppies and 20 Dalmatians adults were used during filming.

11.   The sequel, 101 Dalmatians 2: Patch's London Adventure, was released in 2003. As the Dalmatians are moving house, Patch decides to follow his idol; a celebrity dog called Thunderbolt. Also, Cruella De Vil wants to capture the puppies to paint a canvas with their bodies. Even by evil Disney villain standards, that's pretty messed up.

12.   Someone counted all the black spots in the film, frame-by-frame and reached the grand total of 6,469,952.

13.   The film won a BAFTA for Best Animated Film.

14.   In Germany, the title translates into Pongo and Perdita.

15.   The tagline is, "It's 'arf comedy... 'arf mystery... and it's howlarious!"

16.   The film is based on the 1956 novel, The Hundred and One Dalmatians. It is also known as The Great Dog Robbery. In the book's sequel, the dogs meet aliens and learn how to fly.

A Bug's Life
1998

17.   A Bug's Life was directed by Andrew Stanton and John Lasseter. When they heard that DreamWorks was making a film about ants (called Antz,) Lasseter and Stanton thought DreamWorks were making this film and they were about to be fired.

18.   Hopper's gestures were modelled after Steve Jobs.

19.   The pizza van from Toy Story can been seen straight after the circus scene.

20.   This is the first Pixar film to have outtakes.

21.   The film's trailer has scenes which aren't in the film. This became a Pixar trademark.

22.   Robert De Niro turned down the role of Hopper. The role went to Kevin Spacey.

23.   Hayden Panettiere voices Dot. She is best-known for playing Claire the cheerleader in Heroes.

24.   A short film was shown in the cinemas just before A Bug's Life called Geri' Game.

25.   Joe Ranft voices Heimlich the caterpillar. Ranft also voices Jacques in Finding Nemo and Wheezy in Toy Story 2. On top of that, he was the writer of The Lion King.

26.   The tagline is, "An epic of minitature proportions."

27.   Many people find it silly that two computer-generated films about ants came out in the same year. But they are wrong.
      In 1998, there were THREE computer-generated films about ants! A rip-off of A Bug's Life called Bug Bites: An Ant's Life was made to capitalise on the success of the Pixar film. Bug Bites was only 25 minutes long and has one of the lowest ratings of any film on IMDb (Internet Movie Database.)

A Christmas Carol
2009

28.   The story is based in 1843.

29.   This story involves a lot of time-travel. This film was directed by Robert Zemeckis, who directed Back to the Future, which also revolved around time-travel. Christopher Lloyd and Michael J. Fox, who starred in Back to the Future, were considered for Scrooge. The role went to Jim Carrey.
     Carrey also plays The Ghost of Christmas Past, The Ghost of Christmas Present, and The Ghost of Christmas Future.

30.   Gary Oldman and Lesley Manville play Mr. and Mrs. Cratchit. They were married in real life.

31.   Scrooge is 57.

32.   Gary Oldman plays Marley, Bob Cratchit and Tiny Tim.

33.   A picture of Charles Dickens can be seen in the Cratchit home above the fireplace.

34.   The film cost a whopping $200 million. It made $325 million at the box office.

35.   Cary Elwes plays Dick Wilkins. Robin Wright plays Fan and Belle. They played the main characters in the film, The Princess Bride.

36.   Although scenes were added that were not in the original story, most of the dialogue is word-for-word the same as the Dickens' classic.

A Goofy Movie
1995

37.   The CEO of Disney, Jeffrey Katzenberg, was working so hard during the 1990s, he barely saw his daughter. This encouraged him to make a film about a father taking a road trip with his child to bring them closer together. This concept turned into A Goofy Movie.

38.   Rob Paulsen voices Pete's son, PJ. He has never seen the film.

39.   Steve Martin was considered for the role of Goofy.

40.   In the original script, Goofy and Max were going to compete on a game show called America's Funniest Gladiators.

41.   Donald Duck was supposed to play a pivotal role as a travel agent.

42.   Originally, Pete was going to play a more significant role. He would be on a road trip in a gigantic truck, taunting Goofy everywhere he goes. This concept was taken from Steven Spielberg's film, Duel.

43.   The tagline is "It's the story of a father who couldn't be closer... to driving his son crazy."

44.   Bizarrely, The Lion King was supposed to come out in 1995 and A Goofy Movie was going to come out in 1994. When A Goofy Movie was delayed, The Lion King was rushed for release a year early. That's right. The Lion King came out a year early and it's STILL the best Disney film ever!

The Addams Family
2019

45.　　The story was inspired by a comic strip created by Charles Addams. Most of the characters in the comic strip were unnamed.

46.　　Fester barely appeared in the comic.

47.　　Wednesday Addams' name references the nursery rhyme, Wednesday's Child is Full of Woe.

48.　　Gomez was originally going to be called Repelli. Pugsley was going to be called Pubert.

49.　　Snoop Dogg provides the voice of Cousin Itt.

50.　　Oscar Isaac provides the voice of Gomez. Charlize Theron provides the voice of Morticia. Although they play a married couple, the actors didn't meet until after the film wrapped.

51.　　As soon as the trailer was released, viewers criticised Gomez's horrid appearance since the character is depicted as handsome in previous films and television series.
　　　　However, every character in the film is based on their designs in the original comics. Gomez's appearance is based on Peter Lorre who played Cairo in The Maltese Falcon. Morticia is modelled off Gloria Swanson, who played Norma in Sunset Blvd.

52.　　The tree is called Ichabod. It is named after the main character in Sleepy Hollow, Ichabod Crane.

53.　　This is the first animated adaption where Pugsley is voiced by a child.

54.　　The film was meant to be in stop-motion.

55.　　In Mexico, Thing's name is Fingers, Gomez is called Homero, Uncle Fester is called Lucas, Pugsley is called Pericles, and Wednesday is called Merlina.

56.　　Wednesday's pigtails are shaped like nooses.

The Adventures of Ichabod and Mr. Toad
1949

57.   The film is split into two parts; The first part revolves around Mr. Toad from The Wind in the Willows. The second part revolves around Ichabod Crane from The Legend of Sleepy Hollow.

58.   The Legend of Sleepy Hollow takes place in 1790. The Wind in the Willows takes place in 1909-1910.

59.   The Headless Horseman is so scary, Disney still receive complaints about him to this day.

60.   J. Pat O' Malley voices Cyril. O' Malley also voices Jasper in 101 Dalmatians and Hathi in The Jungle Book.

61.   It took eight years to make this film.

62.   The film was nearly called Two Fabulous Characters.

63.   Ichabod's horse is called Gunpowder.

64.   Ichabod Crane's body is designed to look like a crane bird.

65.   Ichabod is named after a Biblical character. In the Bible, Ichabod is said to mean "inglorious" because he was born on a day of military defeat.

66.   Ichabod Crane is described as looking like a scarecrow. Ichabod was the inspiration for the Batman supervillain, the Scarecrow. Scarecrow's real name is Jonathan Crane.

67.   Basil Rathbone narrates Toad's story. He is best-known for playing Sherlock Holmes in over ten films during the 1940s.

68.   Brom Bones' real name is Abraham Van Brunt. He is named after the Biblical character, Abraham. "Abraham" means "exalted father."

69.   Brom Bones inspired the character of Gaston in Beauty and the Beast.

The Adventures of Tintin: The Secret of the Unicorn
2011

70.　　　　This is the first animated film directed by Steven Spielberg. It was also the first 3D film and first comic book adaptation he directed.

71.　　　　The story is based on three of the Tintin comics – The Crab with the Golden Claws, The Secret of the Unicorn, and Red Rackham's Treasure.

72.　　　　Andy Serkis plays Haddock. Jack Nicholson was considered for the role.

73.　　　　Andy Serkis said the Tintin comics have the same style as the Monty Python films.

74.　　　　This is the first animated film to win a Golden Globe for Best Picture that wasn't made by Pixar.

75.　　　　When Raiders of the Lost Ark came out, Spielberg noticed that a lot of reviews compared the film to the Tintin comics. Out of curiosity, Spielberg decided to read the comic series. He fell in love with the stories and tried for decades to turn it into a movie.

76.　　　　The painter in the beginning is based on the creator of Tintin, Herge.

77.　　　　Jamie Bell plays Tintin. Leonardo DiCaprio was considered for the role.

78.　　　　Tintin is 18.

79.　　　　The story takes place in 1955.

80.　　　　Steven Spielberg intended the film to be live-action. When he contacted Peter Jackson to see if he could use his special effects team, Jackson convinced Spielberg that the film couldn't work in live-action. The directors decided to team up to make a computer-generated Tintin film.

81.   Roman Polanski wanted to direct the film.

82.   Daniel Craig plays Red Rackham. Toby Jones plays Silk. Both of them worked together in Infamous.

83.   The film cost $135 million. Although the director thought the film would be a major success, it only made $374 million, which was considered a small profit. The film didn't do well in the US since the comics are not very well-known outside Europe.

84.   Steven Spielberg always looks at his scenes with one eye closed to visualise the image in 2D. He didn't do this with this film because it is in 3D.

85.   Many directors including Robert Zemeckis, David Fincher, and James Cameron visited the set.

86.   Simon Pegg and Nick Frost play Thompson and Thomson. Both actors worked together in Shaun of the Dead, Hot Fuzz, and The World's End.

87.   It only took Spielberg 31 days to shoot the film.

88.   Peter Jackson stood in for Haddock during test-screening. Spielberg thought Jackson was an excellent Haddock.

Akira
1988

89.   The film is based on a 2,500-page manga comic book. Since the comic is so gigantic, the film only deals with a very small portion of the story.

90.   50 colours were used for Akira that had never been used for an animated film.

91.   The main character is called Kanaeda. In the Japanese version, his name is pronounced "Canada." It's pronounced "Ka-nay-da" in the English dub because Western viewers found it silly that the main character's name sounded like the country, Canada.

92.   The manga was so successful, it was translated into English by Marvel Comics. This is one of the first times in history that a non-English comic series was completely translated into English.

93.   This was directed by Katsuhiro Otomo. He was the writer of the original manga.

94.   This was the most expensive animated film made at the time in Japan, costing $10 million.

95.   The Wachowski brothers said Akira was the biggest influence for their film, The Matrix. When Akira was re-released in 2001, its tagline was, "No Akira, No Matrix."

96.   The film was released two years after the manga concluded.

97.   The film had 738 storyboard pages. The director also wrote 2,000 pages worth of ideas.

98.   Leonardo DiCaprio bought the rights to make a live-action version of the story.

99.   The film contains 2,212 shots and 160,000 single pictures, which is three times more than an average animated film.

Aladdin
1992

100. The man who introduces the film is the Genie. Not only does he have the same beard and clothes as the Genie but they are both voiced by Robin Williams.

101. This was the first film where the advertisements emphasised one of the actors as a selling point.

102. The directors turned down the opportunity to make Beauty and the Beast to direct this film.

103. Robin Williams improvised 16 hours of material for his role as the Genie. He improvised so many lines that the film got turned down for a Best Adapted Screenplay Oscar nomination.

104. Jonathan Freeman voices Jafar. The role nearly went to Patrick Stewart and Ian McKellen.

105. Jonathan Freeman went on to play Jafar on Broadway.

106. Jafar's sidekick is Iago the parrot. Ironically, Jonathan Freeman is scared of parrots.

107. The tagline is "It is not what is outside, but what is inside that counts."

108. The Genie makes over 70 transformations including Jack Nicholson, Rodney Dangerfield, Groucho Marx, Arnold Schwarzenegger, and Robert De Niro. He also did impressions of George Bush and John Wayne but these were cut.

109. Since the Genie makes many references to modern times, some Disney fans theorize that the story doesn't take place in the past but in the far distant future.

110. Most of the characters are drawn with curves. The only main character that isn't drawn with curves is Jafar. Jafar is drawn with straight lines and angles to show that he is the villain since his design doesn't fit with the rest of the characters.

111.   Originally, the lamp in the Cave of Wonders was going to be a fake. When Aladdin rejected it, the real lamp would appear.

112.   Although it is not stated where Agrabah is situated, the inhabitants are Muslim since many of them refer to Allah.

113.   Disney studios were getting tired of generic princesses instantly falling in love with princes and wanted this film to show how and why Jasmine fell in love with Aladdin.

114.   The Beast from Beauty and the Beast can be seen on the Sultan's tower of animals.

115.   Robin Williams' goodbye is very similar to his farewell in the film, Good Morning, Vietnam.

116.   Rajah the tiger tears Prince Achmed's trousers, revealing his underpants. However, Rajah has a torn piece of Achmed's underpants in his mouth, not his trousers.

117.   When the Genie sings, Friend Like Me, he mentions "Scheherazade had her thousand tales." Scheherazade was the story-teller of A Thousand and One Arabian Nights. One of these stories was Aladdin.

118.   Aladdin's movements and pants are based on MC Hammer from his music video, You Can't Touch This.

119.   When Aladdin wants Rajah to back off, he mutters, "Take off, scat, go." Many people believe he says, "Take off your clothes."

120.   Originally, Jafar and Iago's personalities were reversed. Jafar was prone to tantrums while Iago stayed calm.

121.   When the animators didn't know how to jump from one shot to another, they would show Iago getting hurt. Their motto was, "When in doubt, hurt the bird."

122.   This is the first animated Disney film where the main characters were not trained singers. Disney execs worried that

the film would fail because the main actors weren't voiced by professional singers.

123.   The film only cost $28 million. It made a whopping $504 million at the box office. After the film became the most successful film of 1992, executives realised that celebrity actors could boost their films' success. This is the main reason why so many celebrities voiced characters in future Disney films.

124.   Aladdin rolls an apple down his shoulder and flicks it with his elbow. The animators wanted to watch somebody do this so they could animate it properly. None of the film crew were able to do it.

125.   In an early script, there were two Genies; one Genie was in a lamp and the other was in a ring. In this version, the Genie could grant infinite wishes.

126.   The original script was written by Linda Woolverton. Woolverton wrote the screenplay for Beauty and the Beast.

127.   The Carpet was difficult to animate since it couldn't display emotion with speech or facial expressions. The animators studied Charlie Chaplin to learn how a character displays emotion without talking.

128.   The director said that Jafar was based on the former First Lady, Nancy Reagan.

129.   In the original script, Aladdin recognised Jasmine as the princess as soon as he saw her. This was changed as the writers thought it would be better if Aladdin fell in love with her, not knowing of her heritage.

130.   When the Genie frees Aladdin from the Cave of Wonders, Genie calls him "Mr Doubting Mustafa." This is a reference to the idiom "doubting Thomas." Also, Mustafa is the name of Aladdin's father in the original story.

131.   During the Genie's song, he mentions Ali Baba and the Forty Thieves. The second sequel, Aladdin and the King of Thieves, revolves around this legend.

132.   Jasmine's character is the opposite of how she was depicted in the original script. In the first draft, Jasmine was a spoilt brat who wanted to find the richest prince possible.

133.   During the Whole New World scene, Aladdin and Jasmine fly over Japan and Greece. The designs of the buildings were used again for the films, Hercules and Mulan.

134.   Robin Williams had a massive falling out with Disney and he refused to return for the sequel, The Return of Jafar. Disney eventually apologised to Robin Williams and he agreed to return as the Genie in the sequel, Aladdin and the King of Thieves.

135.   The film spawned a television show in 1994. Since Robin Williams didn't want anything to do with it, Dan Castellaneta voices the Genie. Castellaneta is most famous for voicing Homer Simpson in The Simpsons.

136.   In the original script, the story revolved around Aladdin's relationship with his mother. She desperately wanted Aladdin to stop living as a thief but he kept getting encouraged by his friends.

Alice in Wonderland
1951

137.   The film is based on two of Lewis Carroll's books – Alice's Adventures in Wonderland and Through the Looking Glass. Alice's Adventures in Wonderland was written in 1865. Through the Looking Glass was written in 1871.

138.   This film has 14 songs. This is more than any other animated Disney film. Originally, 30 songs were written for the film.

139.   The film was in development for ten years. It took another five years to make. Sadly, Alice in Wonderland made very little money and nearly bankrupted Walt Disney. Disney believed the film failed because Alice wasn't a sympathetic character. Many critics said the film "Americanised" an English classic.

140.   Ed Wynn voices the Mad Hatter. He also played Uncle Albert in Mary Poppins.

141.   The film was supposed to have a mix of live-action, much like Mary Poppins or Bedknobs and Broomsticks.

142.   The Mad Hatter is simply called The Hatter in the novel.

143.   The White Rabbit's watch always says 1225.

144.   The tagline is "'Tis brillig." (It makes sense if you watch the film."

145.   Kathryn Beaumont voices Alice. She dressed as the character while recording her lines.

146.   This was the first Disney film to depict smoking in a negative light. When the Caterpillar blows smoke into Alice's face, she coughs. When smoke was blown into the face of characters in previous Disney movies like Pinocchio or Dumbo, it had no effect.

147.   In the original book, most of the animals look realistic.

148.   Some readers of the original book believe the Queen of Hearts is based on Queen Victoria.

149.   The phrase "mad as a march hare" is based on the fact the march hares become erratic during breeding season and will jump vertically for no reason and attack other rabbits.

150.   Some critics believe the Carpenter is based on Jesus.

151.   Although this is the definitive version of Alice's Adventures in Wonderland, it was the 13th adaptation of Lewis Carrol's book. The first adaptation was a silent eight-minute film in 1903.

152.   There are a few misconceptions about Tweedledee and Tweedledum. Lewis Carroll didn't create these characters. They are nursery rhyme characters that first appeared in stories in 1805.
         Also, the characters weren't in Alice's Adventures in Wonderland. They didn't show up until the sequel.
         The film depicts the Tweedles as twins. This is never referenced in the book.

153.   The original story was nearly called Alice's Adventures Under Ground, Alice Among the Fairies, and Alice's Golden Hour.

154.   The phrase "mad as a hatter" is derived from how mercury was used to make hats in the 19th century. This caused the wearer to suffer mercury poisoning which caused them to suffer amnesia, involuntarily shaking, and slurred speech. Those who suffered mercury poisoning were assumed to be insane.

155.   Many viewers wonder why the Hatter's hat says 10/6 on the side. In the book, The Nursery Alice, it is revealed that this number is simply the price of the hat -10 shillings and six pence.

156.   Many people believe the story is an allusion to hallucinogenic drugs. However, Lewis Carroll wrote Alice's Adventures in Wonderland to show how absurd mathematics is.

157.   Lewis Carroll's real name is Charles Lutwidge Dodgson.

158. Jerry Colonna voices the March Hare. He also voices the Ringmaster in Pinocchio.

159. The only character that is in the original story that wasn't in the film was Mock Turtle. The Doorknob is the only character in the film that wasn't in the original story.

160. Kathryn Beaumont was 13 when she voiced Alice in this film. She reprised her role in the video game, Kingdom Hearts, over half a century later.

161. The Dodo is based on Lewis Carroll. Like Carroll, the Dodo has a stutter in the novel. When Carroll said his surname, it sounded like "Dodogson."

162. Lewis Carroll wrote a poem called Jabberwocky which revolved around a monster called the Jabberwock. Although it was supposed to appear in this film, it was scrapped as Disney thought the monster was too scary.

163. The Queen of Hearts in the film is based on the character of the same name in Alice's Adventures in Wonderland and The Red Queen in Through the Looking Glass.

164. The March Hare is called Haigha.

165. The Drink Me bottle was originally going to speak.

166. Alice changes in size when she drinks or eats certain things in Wonderland. Lewis Carroll came up with this idea while he suffered from migraines. Sometimes his headaches were so severe, objects looked smaller or larger than they were.

167. Lewis Carroll didn't invent the Cheshire Cat character. The phrase "grins like a Cheshire cat" has been found in a 1788 dictionary.

All Dogs Go to Heaven
1989

168.   The film was made by Don Bluth. He used to be a Disney animator.

169.   The title is based on a quote by Robert Louis Stevenson, "You think those dogs will not be in heaven? I tell you they will be there long before any of us."

170.   Burt Reynolds voices the lead, Charlie B. Barkin.

171.   Judith Barsi voices the female lead, Anne-Marie. She was murdered shortly after she recorded her lines. She was only ten years old when she was killed.

172.   Near the end of the film, a big-lipped alligator called King Gator suddenly appears with no explanation. He doesn't fit the context of the story nor does he advance the plot.
         When YouTube vlogger, The Nostalgia Critic, discussed this scene, he coined the term, Big Lipped Alligator Moment when referencing a movie scene that comes out of nowhere. The term, Big Lipped Alligator moment, is now often used to reference nonsensical scenes in movies.

Anastasia
1997

173.   "Anastasia" means "resurrection."

174.   The puppy is called Pooka. In Irish mythology, a pooka is a shape-shifter that brings good luck.

175.   Christopher Lloyd voices Rasputin. The character was nearly voiced by Tim Curry, Jonathan Pryce, and Patrick Stewart.

176.   During the song, Learn to Do It, someone mentions Uncle Vanya. Uncle Vanya is a popular play in Russia written by Anton Chekhov.

177.   Kelsey Grammar voices Vlad. This is the first animated film he worked on.

178.   The director didn't like the final design of Vlad.

179.   Meg Ryan voices Anastasia. Kirsten Dunst voices her as a young girl.

180.   Angela Lansbury voices Empress Marie.

181.   Jim Cummings provides Rasputin's singing voice. Cummings is so good at imitating Christopher Lloyd's voice, most people don't realise it's sung by a different person.

The Angry Birds Movie
2016

182.   Peter Dinklage voices Mighty Eagle. Dinklage is best-known for playing Tyrion in Game of Thrones.

183.   Josh Gad voices Chuck. He originally turned down the role since he didn't want to play another wacky animated character after he voiced Olaf in Frozen.

184.   This is the third time that Gad has worked with Peter Dinklage.

185.   Gad had to speak so fast as Chuck that he needed physical therapy after each recording.

186.   The film was released on July 1st 2016. It was moved to May 20th 2016 to avoid competing against The BFG and The Legend of Tarzan.

187.   Red asks two birds to rate his birthday cake out of three stars. This is a reference to the Angry Birds game where the highest score is three stars.

188.   Parody posters were released to advertise the film. Some of these parodies include Inside Snout (Inside Out,) Redpool (Deadpool,) and The Pig Short (The Big Short.)

189.   On the pig's ship, there is a book called 50 Shades of Green on the bookshelf.

190.   Leonard only refers to Red as "Eyebrows."

191.   There's a Calvin Klein poster on Piggy Island that reads Calvin Swine.

192.   Danny McBride voices Bomb. To get into the head of a character that could explode at any point, McBride claimed that he ate a LOT of burritos.

193.   Sean Penn voices Terence. Terence has no dialogue. He just grumbles, hums, and sings.

The Angry Birds Movie 2
2019

194.   The Angry Birds Movie came out the same year as The Secret Life of Pets. Weirdly, both sequels came out the same year.

195.   The tagline is, "This summer, winter is coming."

196.   The characters of Leslie Jones and Peter Dinklage rekindle their love. This is a reference to a sketch the actors performed on Saturday Night Live.

197.   An eagle guard can be seen reading Crazy Rich Avians. This is a reference to the film, Crazy Rich Asians. Awkwafina, who plays Courtney, starred in Crazy Rich Asians.

Animal Farm
1954

198.   The film is based on George Orwell's novel which was published in 1945. The head of the CIA, E. Howard Hunt, bought the film rights from Orwell's widow, Sonia. Hunt was directly involved in the Watergate scandal that forced Richard Nixon to resign from the American presidency.

199.   Sonia Orwell only agreed to sell the rights under the condition that she could meet her idol, Clark Gable.

200.   In the original novel, the pigs betray the other animals and join forces with the humans. This ending was considered too depressing so it was changed.

201.   This was the first British animated film ever.

202.   Maurice Denham voices every character.

The Animatrix
2003

203.　　This film revolves around the origins of the background and sides-stories of The Matrix. The film was released several weeks after The Matrix Reloaded.

204.　　The Animatrix is made of nine shorts –

i)　　The Second Renaissance Part I – A summary of how the machines turned against humanity.

ii)　　The Second Renaissance Part II – A summary of how the machines built The Matrix.

iii)　　Kid's Story – A tale about the first person who consciously exited the Matrix.

iv)　　A Detective Story – A private detective is tasked with tracking down the computer hacker, Trinity.

v)　　Final Flight of the Osiris – A 3D short that shows what happened to the crew who discovered the army of Squiddies drilling to Zion.

vi)　　Program – A man who lives in Zion who decides to return to living inside The Matrix.

vii)　　Beyond – A group of kids discover an area that "glitches" in The Matrix.

viii)　　World Record – An athlete commits an unprecedented incident by running faster than he physically should be capable of by bending the rules of The Matrix program.

ix)　　Matriculated – A resistance group tries to reprogram a sentinel.

205.　　In The Matrix Reloaded, one of the main Zionists is referred to as Kid. In Kid's Story, it is revealed that his name is Michael Popper.

206.　　The Final Flight of the Osiris takes place moments before The Matrix Reloaded begins.

207.　　Tom Kenny voices the Operator. Kenny voices the titular character in the animated series, SpongeBob Squarepants.

208.　　The Name Plate on the Osiris reads, "Mark IV 16: OSIRIS: Made in the USA 2097." In the Bible, Mark IV 16 reads, "John, the man I beheaded, has been raised from the Dead." Osiris was the

Egyptian god of the afterlife and could raise mortals back from the dead.

209.   The tagline is "Free your mind."

210.   In The Matrix, Morpheus tells Neo that it is unknown whether the humans or the machines struck first.

It is revealed in The Second Renaissance Part I, that a servant robot kills his owners after he learned they were going to dispose of him for a better model. To ensure this didn't happen again, humanity discontinued this model permanently.

When a pair of robots made a peace offering to The United Nations to show that they bared no ill will to humanity, the machines were detained. The machines saw this rejection as an act of war. This began the war between humanity and the machines.

Antz
1998

211.   This is DreamWorks' first animated film.

212.   Arnold Schwarzenegger turned down the role of Weaver. It went to Sylvester Stallone.

213.   Antz cost $105 million. It only made $172 million at the box office.

214.   The film's competition was A Bug's Life. However, Antz had the advantage since it came out a month early. However, the film bombed while A Bug's Life nearly tripled its budget.

215.   Christopher Walken was only meant to have a small part but he was so entertaining when he recorded his lines that his role was expanded.

216.   Dan Aykroyd voices Chip. Bill Murray was considered for the role. Weirdly, both actors starred in Ghostbusters.

217.   This was the second computer-animated film ever. The first was Toy Story.

218.   The film depicts a war against ants and termites. Although termites are shown to be superior, ants would win in a fight as they would easily outnumber the termites.

219.   Woody Allen did all his dialogue as Z in five days.

220.   The story is loosely based on Aldous Huxley's, Brave New World.

The AristoCats
1970

221.   The film was inspired by a real group of Parisian cats who inherited an enormous fortune in 1910.

222.   The story was intended to be a two-part live-action television series.

223.   The Chinese Cat's lines in Ev'rybody Wants to Be A Cat were removed from the soundtracks for being politically incorrect.

224.   Eva Gabor voices Duchess. Phil Harris voices O' Malley. They died one month apart in 1995.

225.   The budget was $4 million. The AristoCats went on to make $35 million at the box office.

226.   The dogs, Napoleon and Lafayette, are named after the French generals, Napoleon Bonaparte and Marquis De Lafayette.

227.   Maurice Chevalier came out of retirement to sing the title song. It was his last work before he passed away two years later.

228.   The tagline is "Get with the cats who know where it's at."

229.   When the kittens are drinking cream in the beginning scene, the coloured ring on each bowl matches the colour of the feline's collar.

230.   This was the first film completed by the Disney studio after Walt Disney's death.

Atlantis: The Lost Empire
2001

231.   Marc Okrand created the Atlantean language. He also invented the Vulcan and Klingon languages in Star Trek. Speaking of which...

232.   Leonard Nimoy voices King Kashekim. He's best-known for playing Spock in Star Trek.

233.   The crew wore t-shirts that read, "Fewer songs, more explosions."

234.   This is one of the only Disney films that says what year it takes place in – 1914.

235.   This was directed by Gary Trousedale and Kirk Wise. They also directed Beauty and the Beast and The Hunchback of Notre Dame.

236.   Kida is the first Disney princess to become a queen.

237.   The animators thought it was clichéd to design Atlantis as "crumbled Greek columns underwater." Because of this, they drew Atlantis so it resembled Mayan buildings.

238.   Milo mentions that Shepherd's journal suddenly stops as if there's a page missing. This is a reference to Plato's stories, Timaeus and Critias, where the story cuts off, as if the rest of the pages have been ripped out.

239.   The tagline is "In a single day and night of misfortune, the island of Atlantis disappeared into the depths of the sea." This quote is from Plato, who devised the story of Atlantis.

240.   Disney made three episodes of an Atlantis series. When the series wasn't picked up, Disney decided to turn the three episodes into the sequel, Atlantis: Milo's Return.

Balto
1995

241.   The film is based on the true story of a husky called Balto who led his team to a village called Nome. The inhabitants were gripped with diphtheria and desperately needed to be inoculated. When Balto reached Nome, the team inoculated the people with an antitoxin. Balto is perceived as a hero since his actions led to an entire town being saved.

However, Balto did not run the longest part nor the most hazardous part of the journey. Of the 20 mushers on this journey, Seppala's husky, Togo, ran further than any other dog on the expedition, at a staggering 260 miles. The reason why Balto got the credit is because he ran the final 55 miles.

Seppala was so angry that his dog didn't receive credit for the expedition that he didn't invite Balto or his owner to Togo's award ceremony in New York.

242.   In the film, Balto is a wolf hybrid. In real life, Balto was a purebred Siberian husky.

243.   Kevin Bacon voices Balto.

244.   Phil Collins voices Muk and Luk. They are named after a type of Canadian shoe called mukluks.

245.   The film spawned the sequels, Balto: Wolf Quest and Balto III: Wings of Change.

246.   The tagline is "Part dog. Part wolf. All hero."

247.   Although the film received positive reviews, it tanked at the box office because it came out the same time as Toy Story.

248.   The Serum Run that Balto committed is known as the Iditarod.

249.   Balto doesn't speak in the last 15 minutes of the film.

Bambi
1942

250.   This was Walt Disney's favourite of all his movies.

251.   The film is based on the 1923 story, Bambi, A Life in the Woods. Although Bambi is one of the most famous Disney films, the novel is not a children's book. It's 293 pages long and contains gore, lust, and murder.

252.   The book was written by an Austrian Jew called Felix Salten. He fled from Austria in 1938 after it was taken over by the Nazis. He died in Switzerland in 1945. Since the book was written by a Jew, it was banned in Nazi Germany for years. Felix Saten sold the rights of his novel to Disney for $1,000.

253.   The novel's sequel, Bambi's Children, The Story of a Forest Family, was released in 1939.

254.   In the novel, Bambi is a roe deer, not a white-tailed deer.

255.   The film was nearly made into a live-action film.

256.   This was the first mainstream animated film where children did the voices of the young characters.

257.   Frank Thomas was the artist who drew Bambi. He also designed Lady Tremaine, Pinocchio, the Seven Dwarfs, Captain Hook, and the Red Queen.

258.   It took six years to make this film.

259.   12 minutes was cut from the film.

260.   Thumper the rabbit and Flower the skunk are not mentioned in the original novel.

261.   Thumper was originally called Bobo.

262.   Two asteroids have been named Bambi and Thumper.

263.   Henry Fonda was considered for the titular role.

264.   In the film, Diamonds Are Forever, James Bond battles two women called Bambi and Thumper, who were named after the characters in this movie.

265.   Humans are never seen in the film.

266.   Several zoos allowed Disney crewmembers to borrow skunks, squirrels, and fawns so the animators could study their movements. After the fawns grew up, they were released into a nearby park.

267.   The animators said that the hardest thing to animate were the antlers of Bambi's father.

268.   In the novel, Faline has a twin brother called Gobo. A man finds Gobo while he is wounded and nurses him back to health before releasing him back into the wild. Later in the story, Gobo walks up to a hunter, believing that humans are not to be feared. Sadly, the hunter shoots Gobo dead.

269.   The deer that Bambi fights is called Ronno.

270.   While making the film, "Man is in the forest" was a code that Disney employees used when Walt Disney was coming down the hallway.

271.   Animation was recycled from Snow White and the Seven Dwarfs to animate Thumper. Some scenes of the woodland creatures and forest fire are unused footage from the film, Pinocchio.

272.   This was the first Disney film where none of the songs were sung by any of the characters.

273.   The film was cleaned up when it was released on DVD. Many viewers don't understand how much work it takes to clean up the negatives of an old film. Disney filmmakers spent 9,600 hours cleaning the negatives (over a year) to make them look as sharp as possible.

274.   Originally, Bambi was going to be shot, not his mother.

275.   Originally, Bambi was supposed to run up to his dead mother after she is shot.

276.   Walt Disney decided not to show the hunter as he worried that children would assume all hunters are evil.

277.   Donnie Dunagan voices Young Bambi. He became a Marine and the youngest drill instructor in history and eventually became a Major in the Vietnam War. He never told anyone that he voiced Bambi during the war, afraid that he would get bullied.

278.   In the original script, the hunter was supposed to die in the forest fire. This would show Bambi that humans were not all-powerful.

279.   The original story is considered to be one of the first environmental novels.

280.   The film cost $1.7 million. The film only made $1.64 million at the box office. The film didn't do well because it wasn't released in Japan or Europe for years due to WWII. This was the last animated Disney film for eight years because most of animators were in the military during the war.

281.   The animation from this film has been recycled more than any other Disney cartoon. Shots of birds flying, leaves blowing, forest animals sleeping, etc. have been used in other films including The Sword in the Stone, The Jungle Book, and The Rescuers.

282.   Bambi II was released in 2006. This means there is a gap of 64 years between the original and the sequel, which is the world record.

283.   When America Film Institute ranked the 100 greatest heroes and villains, the murderer of Bambi's mother (simply known as Man,) was ranked #20. He was the only person on the list that never appeared onscreen.

Beauty and the Beast
1991

284.   The Prince was 11 years old when the Enchantress turned him into the Beast.

285.   Andeas Deja designed Gaston. He also designed Jafar from Aladdin and Scar in The Lion King.

286.   The roars that Beast makes are from a mountain lion.

287.   Walt Disney tried to make this film during the 1930s and the 1950s.

288.   An Eiffel Tower-shaped structure appears in the Be Our Guest scene. However, construction of the Eiffel Tower didn't start until 1887 and the film is set in the 1700s.

289.   Gaston's sidekick is called Le Fou. His name means "idiot" in French.

290.   The tagline is "The most beautiful love story ever told."

291.   In The Mob Song, Gaston sings, "Screw your courage to the sticking place." This is a line from Shakespeare's play, Macbeth.

292.   This was the first animated film to be nominated for a Best Picture Oscar.

293.   Belle's character was inspired by Katherine Hepburn.

294.   This film was so successful, the Oscars created the Best Animated Feature category the following year.

295.   After Gaston proposes to Belle, she runs into a field. This is based on The Sound of Music when Maria sings in a field.

296.   Although it is unknown what book Belle is reading in the beginning, fans suspect it is Sleeping Beauty.

297.   Jackie Chan voices the Beast in the Chinese dub.

298.   In the French version, Cogsworth is called Big Ben. He is named after the London bell which resides in the clock tower in the Palace of Westminster in London.

299.   In the very last shot of Gaston, skulls can be seen in his eyes for a split-second.

300.   Originally, there was going to be a music box character that communicated through musical notes.

301.   Paige O' Hara was in her 30s when she voiced the 17-year-old Belle.

302.   This is Paige O' Hara's first acting credit.

303.   Paige O' Hara has voiced Belle over ten times in video games, films, and television series.

304.   Bambi's mother is drinking from the stream in the opening shot. There is an Internet theory that Gaston is the hunter that killed Bambi's mother.

305.   Belle was supposed to be played by Jodi Benson. Benson voices Ariel in The Little Mermaid.

306.   The actors were encouraged to improvise lines, which is rare for a Disney film.

307.   Most of the characters are voiced by Broadway actors. Disney did this in the hope that they could turn the story into a Broadway musical.

308.   Paige O' Hara sobbed genuine tears when she recorded Belle's final scene. Afterward, the director asked her if she was ok. She shouted, "Acting!"

309.   Belle's blue-and-white dress is based on Dorothy's dress in The Wizard of Oz.

310.   The film inspired a spin-off in 1997 called Beauty and the Beast: The Enchanted Christmas.

311.   When Beast gets a makeover, he says that he looks stupid. His look in this scene is based on the Cowardly Lion from The Wizard of Oz.

312.   The film had another spin-off film in 1998 called Belle's Magical World. It was supposed to be an animated series but it was cancelled after three episodes due to poor animation and storylines. The studio decided to repackage it as a movie to make some money back. It is considered to be the worst animated Disney movie ever.

313.   Jerry Orbach voices Lumiere. He played Lennie in Law & Order for 13 years.

314.   Richard White voices Gaston. He only has five acting credits.

315.   This is one of the first films that Pixar worked on. They animated the chandelier during Belle and Beast's dance.

316.   Although most animated films take four or five years to make, Beauty and the Beast only took two years.

317.   The song, Human Again, was completed but not used for the finished film. It was inserted into the movie when it was released on DVD.

318.   Tony Jay voices the owner of the insane asylum, Monsier D'Arque. The filmmakers said he performed the best audition. He was so good, the director used his audition for the final film so Jay didn't have come in to voice any additional dialogue.

319.   Belles final dance with the Prince is recycled animation from Princess Aurora and Prince Phillip in the film, Sleeping Beauty.

320.   This was the most successful film of the year apart from Terminator 2.

321.   The Beast's appearance is a composition of many animals. He has a bear's body, a boar's tusks, a lion's main, a gorilla's

brow, a buffalo's beard, a human's eyes, and a wolf's tail and legs.

322.   The earliest version of this story is Cupid and Psyche, which was written in the 2nd century by Platonicus. The main character, Lucius, transmogrifies into a donkey after a magic spell goes wrong. He regains his humanity after eating a sacred rose.

323.   Another version of the Beauty and the Beast was The Pig King, which was written by Gianfrancesco in the 16th century. The story revolves around a mother who urges her daughters to marry a king called Marcassin.

Although the daughters are repulsed by Marcassin because he resembles a boar-beast, the mother begs one of them to marry him for his money. This story was written to show the pressure that people in arranged marriages go through.

324.   The most famous version of Beauty and the Beast is the 1756 tale by Jeanne-Marie Leprince de Beaumont. However, there are many differences between this version and the Disney film. In Beaumont's story, the Beast is kind from the very beginning. He does not entice the girl (who is called Beauty) in any way and does not sit with her unless she asks him to. The Beast believes a person of purity will love him for his kindness rather than his appearance.

Bee Movie
2007

325.   Barry and other male bees have stingers. In real life, only female bees have stingers. Also, bees don't make honey in real life.

326.   Jerry Seinfeld voices the lead, Barry B. Benson. The role nearly went to Jason Bateman.

327.   Jerry Seinfeld came up with the title as a joke to Steven Spielberg. Spielberg loved the idea and encouraged Seinfeld to make it into a film.

328.   Renee Zellweger voices Vanessa. Jennifer Lopez was considered for the role.

329.   The story was originally going to be live-action.

330.   The film inspired a rip-off called Plan Bee, which came out the same year.

331.   Sting, Ray Liotta, and Larry King voice themselves.

332.   The tagline is, "Honey just got funny."

333.   The first trailer was in live-action and has Jerry Seinfeld dressed in a bee costume.

334.   John Goodman voices Layton. The role nearly went to James Gandolfini.

335.   Buzzwell is modelled after The Boss from the animated series, Dilbert.

Beowulf
2007

336.   The film is based on the oldest known English story. Beowulf was written between 700-1000 AD.

337.   The actors had to wear motion-capture suits. They had to physically act out all their scenes and then animation was put on top of their movements.

338.   Ray Winstone plays the titular character. He hated wearing his blue skin-tight suit because he was "showing up all your lumps and bumps in all the wrong places. Which can be hard when you're standing in front of Angelina Jolie, who looks stunning in hers."

339.   The monster is called Grendel. He speaks in Old English. This is the same English that the original poem was written in.

340.   Anthony Hopkins plays King Hrothgar. At one point, he says, "Odin be praised." He went on to play Odin in the film, Thor.

341.   Crispin Glover plays Grendel. He has worked with the director, Robert Zemeckis, in Back to the Future.

342.   Beowulf means "Bee-Wolf."

343.   The film required a whopping 300 cameras.

The BFG
1989

344.   The film is based on the 1982 book of the same name. When the writer, Roald Dahl, saw this film, he said he enjoyed it. This is pretty impressive since he detested the film Willie Wonka and the Chocolate Factory, which was based on his novel, Charlie and the Chocolate Factory.

345.   The film was first shown on Christmas Day in 1989 in the UK.

346.   David Jason voices the titular character.

347.   David Jason named his daughter, Sophie. Sophie is the name of the main character in this story.

348.   The boy who dreams of turning invisible has a Danger Mouse poster in his bedroom. David Jason played the titular character in the cartoon, Danger Mouse.

Big Hero 6
2014

349.   Baymax's movements are based on a baby with a full diaper. The Microbots are based on fire ants.

350.   Stan Lee can be seen in a painting in one scene. He cameos in the post-credits scene.

351.   The world that the animators created is bigger than the worlds of Tangled, Wreck-It Ralph, and Frozen combined.

352.   The villain is called Yokai. This means "phantom" in Japanese.

353.   A short called Feast was shown in the cinema before this film.

354.   Honey Lemon is the only character that pronounces Hiro's name correctly.

355.   Hans from Frozen and Flynn from Tangled can be seen on a Wanted sign in the police station. Also, when Baymax tests his rocket, he blows up a statue of Hans.

356.   The hardest thing to animate was Baymax's wings.

357.   The words "Big Hero 6" are never said at any point.

358.   Many people don't know that this story is based on a Marvel comic. However, the film has very little resemblance to the series.

359.   The film is set in San Fransokyo in the year, 2032.

360.   James Cromwell voices Callaghan. His enemy, Krei, is voiced by Alan Tudyk. Both actors starred in another robot themed film, I, Robot.

361.   To challenge the animators, the studio wanted Baymax to have as little animation in his face as possible. Baymax's designers said it felt like "UNimating" instead of "animating."

362.   Jamie Chung voices Gogo. She is Disney's first Korean character.

363.   Scott Adsit voices Baymax. He's best-known for playing Pete Hornberger in 30 Rock.

364.   In the original story, the main villain was Everwraith; a spirit composed of the souls of everyone who died in the nuclear attack on Hiroshima and Nagasaki.

The Black Cauldron
1985

365.   This was the first animated Disney film to have no songs.

366.   Disney studios tried to make the film since 1971.

367.   John Hurt voices the main villain, the Horned King.

368.   The film was suspended from video release for years because it was considered too disturbing for children.

369.   This is the film that Disney is most ashamed of.

370.   Tim Burton was one of the crewmembers. He wanted the Horned King to have lackeys that resembled the Facehuggers from the Alien series.

371.   The Horned King's demise is considered to be the most horrific death in any Disney film.

372.   It took 12 years to make this film.

373.   This was the first Disney film to use the iconic Disney logo in the beginning.

Bolt
2008

374.   The story revolves around a dog called Bolt who stars in a TV show about a canine with superpowers. However, Bolt actually believes he has superpowers and becomes incredibly confused and disillusioned when he gets lost. The film's structure was heavily inspired by The Truman Show, which also revolved around a character who was unaware that he is the star of a show.

375.   In Russia, the film is called Volt. In Poland, the film is called Lightning. In Bulgaria, the film is called Thunder.

376.   The Bolt TV show was supposed to be called The Omega Dog.

377.   The short, Tokyo Mater, was shown in the cinema before this film.

378.   The tagline is "Fully awesome."

379.   John Travolta voices the titular character.

380.   James Lipton voices The Director. Lipton is the host of Inside the Actors Studio.

381.   Malcolm McDowell voices the feline-themed villain, Dr. Calico. A calico is a type of cat.

382.   This was the first film ever released on Blu-Ray before DVD.

Book of Life
2014

383.   Channing Tatum voices Joaquin. Ice Cube voices Candle Maker. They worked together in 21 Jump Street.

384.   The original title was El Matador.

385.   Ron Perlman voices Xibalba. Xibalba is the name of the Underworld according to the Ancient Mayans.

386.   Christian Applegate voices Mary Beth. She is best-known for playing Kelly in Married with Children and Veronica in Anchorman.

387.   The film is called Day of the Dead in the United States.

The Boss Baby
2017

388.   Alec Baldwin voices the titular character. Lisa Kudrow voices Mom. The two actors played a couple in the TV series, Friends.

389.   Tobey Maguire voices the narrator. The part was supposed to go to Patton Oswald.

390.   Miles Bakshi voices Tim. He is the grandson of Ralph Bakshi who directed the 1978 animated film, The Lord of the Rings. As a reference to this fact, Tim has a Gandalf-styled alarm clock.

391.   Jimmy Kimmel voices Dad.

392.   The tagline was, "Ruthless and toothless!"

393.   Steve Buscemi voices Francis Francis. The original choice was Kevin Spacey.

394.   The story is loosely based on a 2010 book of the same name.

395.   At one point, Boss Baby says, "Put that cookie down! Cookies are for closers!" This is a reference to the film, Glengarry Glen Ross, when Alec Baldwin's character shouts, "Put that coffee down! Coffee is for closers!"

396.   Boss Baby's name is Theodore Lindsey Templeton.

The Boxtrolls
2014

397. Simon Pegg voices Herbert. Nick Frost voices Trout. The pair have worked together on many projects including Spaced and Shaun of the Dead. Weirdly, they had no idea that the other was in the film because they recorded their lines separately.

398. 20,000 props were made for the film.

399. Dee Bradley Baker voices Fish, Wheels, and Bucket. He's one of the best voice actors in the world and has starred in over 450 projects. He also helped developed the boxtroll language.

400. Elle Fanning voices Winnie. Her sister, Dakota, was the lead of Coraline, which was made by the same stop-motion company, Laika.

401. 330 stop-motion animators worked on the film.

402. The tagline was, "Heroes come in all shapes and sizes... even rectangles."

Brave
2012

403. The short, La Luna, was shown in cinemas before this film.

404. 75% of the dialogue in the film is spoken by females, which is more than any other Disney film.

405. It took Pixar three years to perfect Merida's curly hair.

406. Many viewers complained that the film has an uneven tone as if it has two stories slapped together. This is because the director, Brenda Chapman, was fired after two years and was replaced with Mark Andrews who drastically changed designs and key plot points.

407. Until Mark Andrews took over, 80% of the film took place in the snow.

408. The audience never sees Merida eat anything except apples.

409. Merida is 5ft 4. The bear is 9ft tall. However, their heights were altered if they were in the same scene so they would fit in the shot.

410. Emma Thompson voices Merida's mother, Elinor.

411. Elinor is based on the original director, Brenda Chapman. Merida is based on Chapman's daughter.

412. Merida lives in Caslte DunBroch. The name translates into "Castle Castle Castle."

413. Merida's hair is made of 1,500 curls.

414. John Ratzenberg voices Gordon. He has starred in nearly 20 Pixar films.

415. Billy Connolly voices Fergus. Sean Connery was considered for the role.

416.   "Merida" is Hebrew for "rebel."

417.   Julie Walters voices the Witch. David Tennant was considered for the role.

418.   Robbie Coltrane voices Lord Dingwall. Kelly Macdonald voices Merida. Both actors worked on the Harry Potter series.

419.   The film is dedicated to Steve Jobs who died in 2011.

420.   This film has many firsts in Pixar's history. This is the first Pixar film where the lead is female. Merida is the first Disney princess which is not based on a pre-existing character or historical figure. Merida is the first Disney princess not to have a love interest. She is the first Disney princess to have brothers. Merida is the first Disney princess of Pixar.

421.   The black bear is called Mor'du. It is based on the Gaelic term, "Mor Dubh," which means "large black one."

422.   The original title was The Bear and the Bow.

423.   A film called Super K was expected to be released in 2011. When the creators noticed that the main character in Super K looked similar to Merida in the upcoming Pixar film, Brave, they retitled Super K as Kiara the Brave even though the story has no resemblance to the Pixar film.
        Brave is about a female archer in medieval Scotland. According to IMDb, this is the story of Super K - "King Maximus's Dreamzone empire is threatened by his brother Badmess and Dr. Ozox."

424.   There is a theory that the witch is actually Boo from Monsters, Inc. Now you might think, "That doesn't make any sense! Boo is a toddler in Monsters, Inc. and Brave is set centuries ago! How could you possibly connect the two?" Because the witch has a carving of Boo's friend, Sulley.
        The theory suggests that Boo becomes a witch when she becomes older and eventually time-travels to medieval Scotland where she meets Merida.

Brother Bear
2003

425.   Rick Moranis voices Rutt in this film and the 2006 sequel. He's best-known for Ghostbusters, Spaceballs, and Honey, I Shrunk the Kids. Brother Bear 2 is the last film he has starred in.

426.   Joaquin Phoenix voices the lead, Kenai.

427.   The moose are called Tuke and Rutt. In the German version, they are called Benny and Bjorn. They are named after the two male singers from the Swedish band, ABBA.

428.   The tagline is, "The Moose Are Loose!"

429.   Disney considered making a spin-off show of Tuke and Rutt.

430.   Most of the characters are named after places in Alaska.

431.   Michael Clarke Duncan voices Tug the bear. He played a character called Bear in Armageddon. Tug's appearance and facial expressions were modelled after Michael Clark Duncan.

Captain Underpants: The First Epic Movie
2017

432.   The story is based on Dav Pilkey's book series, The Adventures of Captain Underpants. The series ran from 1997-2015.

433.   The film was supposed to be made in the early 2000s with Chris Farley voicing the titular character. After Farley died, the project was shelved.

434.   The story is based on the first four books.

435.   The tagline was, "Putting the Mighty in Tighty Whitey."

436.   Kevin Hart voices George. Ed Helms voices Captain Underpants. They worked together before in the 2008 film, Meet Dave.

Cars
2006

437. The short, One Man Band, was shown in the cinemas before this film.

438. The original title was Route 66.

439. At the time of its release, this was the longest Pixar film at 117 minutes.

440. Fillmore says that the third blink of the stoplight in Radiator Springs is half a second slower. This is true.

441. All the jets in the sky make tyre marks.

442. Guido's name is Italian for "I drive."

443. The tagline is, "Life is a journey. Enjoy the trip."

444. Paul Newman voices Hudson. He thought this was his best performance in 20 years.

445. The Michael Schumacher Ferrari is actually voiced by Michael Schumacher. Michael Schumacher recorded his lines in English, German, Italian, and French.

446. Michael Keaton voices the villain, Chick Hicks.

447. John Ratzenberger voices Mack, Hamm Truck, PT Flea Car, and the Abominable Snow Plow.

448. George Carlin voices Fillmore. He died three months before the film was released.

449. The film inspired a rip-off called A Car's Life: Sparky's Big Adventure. In had four sequels.

450. A car version of Jay Leno appears called Jay Limo.

451. This was the most successful film of Paul Newman's career.

452.   It took 17 hours to render a single frame of the film even though the animators were using computers a thousand times faster than the ones they had while making Toy Story.

453.   This was the last Pixar film to be released on VHS and the first Pixar film released on Blu-Ray.

454.   Lightning is based on Michael Jordan, Muhammad Ali, and Steve McQueen.

455.   The original script was written in 1999 and was called The Little Yellow Car. The story revolved around an electric car living in a gas-obsessed world.

456.   Luigi's towers of tires lean to one side. This is a reference to The Leaning Tower of Pisa.

457.   The codename for the film was Surgery.

458.   Guido only says three words in the entire film.

459.   The insects are Volkswagen Beetles. This is because this type of car is known as a "Bug."

460.   This is the first Pixar film to use a technique called "ray tracing," which automatically reflects certain surfaces.

461.   The film contains 36 racers.

462.   The story is similar to a 1991 film called Doc Hollywood. Both films revolve around an arrogant character who is sentenced to community to service in a small town after destroying property but eventually falls in love with the place.

463.   This is the last film that Joe Ranft worked on. Ironically, he died in a car crash.

Cars 2
2011

464.   Eddie Izzard voices Miles.

465.   This is the first Pixar film not to be nominated for the Best Animated Feature Oscar.

466.   Michael Caine voices Finn McMissile. He was supposed to appear in the first film.

467.   Cars 2 inspired two spin-offs; Planes in 2013 and Plane: Fire & Rescue in 2014.

468.   The tagline is "Going where no car has gone before."

469.   The drive-in is showing a movie called The Incredimobiles. It is a car version of The Incredibles.

470.   Gusteau's restaurant from Ratotouille appears in Cars under the name Gastows.

471.   Cars 2 is considered to be the worst Pixar film and is the only Pixar feature to receive a Rotten score from the critics at Rotten Tomatoes.

Cars 3
2017

472. The short, LOU, was shown before Cars 3 in the cinema.

473. The film was directed by Brian Fee. This is his directorial debut.

474. Lewis Hamilton voices Hamilton.

475. The film contains 65 different racers.

476. Weirdly, every Cars film came out the same year as a Pirates of the Caribbean film.

477. This is the first Pixar film that wasn't nominated for an Oscar, a Golden Globe, or a BAFTA.

478. The tagline is "It's not over until lightning strikes."

479. Cinderella's carriage can be seen in Sterling's office.

480. Nathan Fillion voices Sterling. This isn't the first Pixar film he has appeared in. Fillion voices Johnny in Monster's University.

481. Lea DeLaria voices Miss Fritter. Lea is best-known for playing Boo in Orange is the New Black.

482. The post-credits scene shows Mater struggling to answer his smartphone.

483. Some of Paul Newman's dialogue that was cut from Cars was used for this film, making this his final performance nine years after he died.

484. This is the least successful film in the trilogy.

485. The Cars trilogy has made over $8 billion in merchandise.

Castle in the Sky
1986

486. The story takes place in the floating castle of Laputa. It's named after the flying island in Jonathan Swift's novel, Gulliver's Travels.

487. The film was originally in Japanese. It wasn't dubbed into English for 13 years.

488. Shita's name was changed to Sheeta for the English dub for... obvious reasons.

489. This was the first film created by Studio Ghibli.

490. Mark Hamill voices Muska.

491. The title was Laputa but it was changed when the director learned that it translated into "slag" in Spanish.

Chicken Little
2005

492.   When Buck Cluck is driving Chicken Little to school, a bull can be seen in a China shop.

493.   Patrick Stewart voices Mr. Woolensworth. This is the first Disney film that Stewart has been a part of. He was offered nine other Disney roles in other Disney films but he was busy shooting Star Trek.

494.   Mark Dindal directed the film. He also directed The Emperor's New Groove.

495.   The tagline is "Who you calling chicken?"

496.   The first few minutes of the story is based on the fable, The Sky is Falling.

497.   Zach Braff voices the titular role.

498.   Chicken Little was going to be a girl.

499.   Adam West voices Ace.

Chicken Run
2000

500.   All the characters are made of silicone with latex covering. The heads, hands, and wings are made of plasticine.

501.   3,370lbs of plasticine was made for the chicken models.

502.   In Russia, the film is called Escape from the Hen House.

503.   The tagline is, "This Ain't No Chick Flick!"

504.   Although the animation was performed in England, Mel Gibson recorded his lines in the US.

505.   When Rocky leaves, Bunty says, "I don't even think he was American." This is a reference to the American actor, Mel Gibson, who is often mistaken as Australian.

506.   The crew had difficulty making Rocky and Ginger kiss since they have beaks. This became a recurring joke so they get interrupted every time they are about to kiss. When they finally kiss, it is obscured so it can't be seen properly.

507.   Mrs. Tweedy's first name is Melisha. It is a reference to the word, "malicious."

508.   It took about a week to make a batch of three chicken models.

509.   Timothy Spall voices Nick. Imelda Staunton voices Bunty. Both actors played villains in the Harry Potter series.

Cinderella
1950

510.   Cinderella's castle is the logo for Disney.

511.   This was the last Disney film released while Walt Disney was still alive.

512.   Cinderella cost $2.9 million. The film originally made over $34 million. Since the film has been re-released over the years, it has accumulated over $93 million.

513.   When the Fairy Godmother creates Cinderella's dress, it's white. For some reason, the dress is blue at the ball.

514.   This was the first successful animated Disney film in 17 years.

515.   Although Disney have confirmed that the prince is called Charming, he is never named at any point in the film.

516.   There could be as many as 1,500 versions of the Cinderella story. In certain versions of the story, Cinderella's slippers are made of gold.
        The oldest version of the Cinderella story is the Egyptian tale, Rhodopis. It was written in the 7th century BC and was adapted by the Greek philosopher, Strabo, in the 1st century.

517.   309 people auditioned for Cinderella. Ilene Woods won the role without auditioning.

518.   The film is made up of 125,000 pictures.

519.   If the film flopped, Walt Disney would've gone bankrupt.

520.   The King and the Grand Duke are voiced by the same person – Luis Van Rooten.

521.   It took six years to make the film.

522.   Although Cinderella has orange hair in this film, she has blonde hair in the sequel.

523.   Cinderella loses her slipper three times.

524.   Many people assume the song, Bibbidi-Bobbidi-Boo, was written for this film. On the contrary, the song was popular before this film was released.

525.   This story is mainly based on the 1697 book, Cendrillon, which was written by Charles Perrault. It was one of the first versions of Cinderella to have a fairy godmother, glass slippers, and a pumpkin carriage.

526.   "Cendrillon" means "Little Ash Girl." This is a reference to the fact that she is covered in soot (or cinders) since she is always cleaning.

527.   The Brothers Grimm version of Cinderella is called Aschenputtel. In this story, Aschenputtel cries over her mother's grave after her stepsisters are nasty to her. Her tears turn into a magical tree, which dresses her in a beautiful gown.
        At the end of the story, the stepsisters chop off their toes and heel to try and fit into the glass slipper. When Aschenputtel gets married, the stepsisters have their eyes pecked out by doves.

528.   The film takes place during the mid-19th century.

529.   Ilene Woods voices Cinderella. As she got older, she suffered Alzheimer's disease and forgot that she was in this film. Nevertheless, she was always comforted by the song, A Dream Is a Wish Your Heart Makes.

530.   Ilene Woods quit acting a year after this film was released.

531.   Helene Stanley was the live-action model for Cinderella. She was also the model for Aurora in Sleeping Beauty.

532.   Cinderella's wicked step-sisters are called Drizella and Anastasia. These names were made up for the film. In most versions of the story, the sisters are unnamed.

533.   Drizella's hair changes from brown to black throughout the film.

534. Cinderella is 19. She was the oldest Disney Princess until the 20-year-old Tiana appeared in The Princess and the Frog.

535. Eleanor Audley voiced Lady Tremaine. She voices Maleficent in Sleeping Beauty.

536. 300 artists worked on the film. If one artist drew every image, it would have taken him 42 years to draw everything.

537. In one script, Cinderella had a turtle called Clarissa.

538. Disney shot the entire film in live action first to highlight gestures and expressions. This saved the animators time so they didn't have to work from scratch. Walt Disney had to do this because he was low on money and animators since most of his original crew were recovering after fighting in World War II. If he didn't use live action, the film would've been three times more expensive.

539. Cinderella was the first Disney princess not to be born into royalty.

540. June Foray voices Lucifer the cat. She also voices Betty in The Flintstones.

541. When Cinderella dances with Prince Charming, their shadows don't match. This is because the animators found it too difficult.

542. The tagline is "The greatest love story ever told."

543. The film spawned a sequel in 2002 called Cinderella II: Dreams Come True. The film had another sequel in 2007 called Cinderella 3: A Twist in Time. In this film, Cinderella's evil step-mother, Lady Tremaine, goes back in time to make sure Cinderella never becomes a princess.

544. Cinderella's shoe size is 4½.

545. Although Cinderella was nominated for three Oscars, the film didn't win anything.

546.　When the Fairy Godmother performs her magic spell on Cinderella, a halo appears above Cinderella's head for a split-second.

547.　There is an urban legend that the slippers were made of squirrel fur in one of the original stories but this isn't true.

548.　The mice's clothes are similar to the dwarves from Snow White and the Seven Dwarfs. Gus' clothes and hat are the same colour as Bashful the Dwarf.

549.　This is not the first Cinderella cartoon made by Disney. Walt Disney made a short cartoon in 1922 simply called Cinderella.

550.　Although Cinderella is one of the most famous fictional princesses ever, she was heavily criticised at the time for being one-dimensional, boring, and passive. Some critics even accused her of being a gold-digger.

551.　Disney decided to remake all of their classic animated films into live action. The 2015 remake, Cinderella, was the first movie to get this treatment.

552.　Walt Disney said that the transformation of Cinderella's dress was the greatest thing his team had ever animated.

Cloudy with a Chance of Meatballs
2009

553.   Mr T. voices Earl Devereaux. Earl's hairstyle is the exact opposite of Mr. T's. Mr. T has a T-shaped hairstyle. Earl has a T-shaped bald patch.

554.   The tagline is, "Prepare to get served."

555.   Bill Hader voices Flint. His lab is based on Nikola Tesla's laboratory.

556.   In Israel, the film is called It's Raining Falafel.

557.   Anna Faris voices Sam Sparks. Amy Poehler nearly voiced the character.

558.   Bruce Campbell voices Mayor Shelbourne. He never met Bill Hader until after the production ended since they recorded their lines separately.

559.   The story is based on the 1978 novel of the same name.

560.   The film had a sequel which revolved around living food called foodimals. The writers came up with 120 puns for the foodimals including Tacodile, Sasquash, Fruit Cockatiel, Shrimpanzee, Flamango, Susheep, Wildebeet, Watermelphant, Lemmongs, and Buffaloaf. Only 39 were used for the final cut.

Coco
2017

561.   "Coco" means "crap" in Portuguese. Because of this, the title was changed to Viva in Brazil and the character of Coco was called Ines.

562.   The film was directed by Lee Unkrich. He also directed Toy Story 3.

563.   The story's structure is heavily based on Back to the Future and The Wizard of Oz.

564.   The Pizza Express truck from Toy Story drives by Miguel's house in the opening scene.

565.   Gael Garcia Bernal voices Hector. He is the only main actor to voice his character in English and Spanish.

566.   Miguel says he'll play guitar "if it kills me." This turns out to be true.

567.   The main character is Miguel. He is the first non-Caucasian human protagonist in a Pixar film.

568.   The dead characters use outdated technology like walkie-talkies and MacIntosh computers.

569.   A poster of Incredibles 2 briefly appears during the firework scene at Ernesto's plaza.

570.   Since Pixar are known for going the extra mile in their details, it won't surprise you to learn that the fingers of the guitar player when they are playing the instrument are always accurate.

571.   Saint Cecilia graveyard is named after the Catholic saint of musicians.

572.   Miguel's grandmother and great-great-grandmother repeatedly hit people with their shoe. This type of shoe is known as a Chancia.

573.   "Coco" is derived from "Socorro" which means "relief."

574.   Ernesto's choreographer is Frida Kahlo. She is one of Mexico's most famous artists of all time.

575.   Dante is a hairless dog called a Xoloitzcuintli. Frida refers to Dante as a spirit animal. This is a reference to the fact that the dog became popular in Mexico after Frida adopted a Xolo.

576.   Frida's papaya show references two of her paintings – Still Life, Round and Last Supper.

577.   Dante is named after the writer of The Divine Comedy, Dante Aligheri. The story revolves around a character who travels to Heaven and Hell, much like how the Xolo dog guides Miguel to The Land of the Dead.

578.   Since the story revolves around Dia de los Muertos, many people accused Pixar of copying the story of the 2014 film, Book of Life, which revolves around the same festival. However, Coco has been in production since 2011 so any similarities the film has with Book of Life is coincidental.

579.   In the original script, the lead character was called Marco.

580.   The film has been in production longer than any other Pixar film. It took so long to make, the actor who portrayed Miguel was recast since he hit puberty and his voice no longer suited the character.

581.   Anthony Gonzalez plays the lead character, Miguel. Although Miguel played the guitar in the original script, he was never meant to sing. The director incorporated this into the script when he learned Gonzalez was a talented singer.

582.   John Ratzenberger cameos in almost every Pixar film. In Coco, he provides the voice of Juan Ortodoncia. He is the skeleton who can cross over to The Land of the Living because his dentist remembers him.

583.   The hardest thing to animate was Abuelita's neck.

584.   The film won an Oscar for Best Animated Feature.
Remember Me won for the Oscar for Best Original Song.

585.   In The Land of the Dead, the colourful houses are stacked
on top of each other. This is inspired by the buildings in the
Mexican city of Guanajuato.

586.   The film made $150 million in five days. It made more in
19 days than Cars 3 did in over five months. It went on to make
$806 million at the box office. Coco was #1 at the box office for
three weeks in the US. It spent more time at #1 at the box office
than any animated film in the 21st century.
     Unsurprisingly, it went on to become the most successful film
in Mexican history.

587.   The heavy metal band is called Escapula, which means
"Shoulder Blade."

588.   This is the ninth Pixar film to win an Oscar for Best
Animated Feature. It is the third Pixar film to win an Oscar for
Best Original Song.

589.   Benjamin Bratt voices Ernesto. This is the fourth
animated film he has starred in since he appeared in Despicable
Me 2 and Cloudy with a Chance of Meatballs 1 and 2.

590.   China have incredibly strict censors and rarely allow a
film to be shown in their country if death plays a major theme.
The Chinese censor board were so touched by this film's
message, they allowed it to be released.

591.   During the credits, a picture of over a hundred deceased
people who inspired the filmmakers appears. Walt Disney's
photo is in the middle.

Coraline
2009

592.   This is the longest stop-motion film ever at 100 minutes.

593.   There's one scene where Coraline shows 16 different expressions in 35 seconds. The animators said this was the hardest part of the film to animate.

594.   This was the first stop-motion film to be shot entirely in 3D.

595.   Originally, the film was going to be live-action.

596.   The tagline is, "Oh. My. God."

597.   The film cost $60 million.

598.   The film was made by the Laika stop-motion animation studio. They also made ParaNorman, The Boxtrolls, and Kubo and the Two Strings.

599.   Dawn French voices Miss Forcible and Jennifer Saunders voices Miss Spink. Originally, they were cast in opposing roles.

600.   It took up to four months and ten individuals to make one puppet of Coraline.

601.   One crewmember knitted clothes for all the characters.

602.   The snow was made from superglue and baking soda.

603.   Coraline was in pre-production for two years.

604.   130 sets were built for the film.

605.   28 puppets were made for the character of Coraline.

606.   The film is based on Neil Gaiman's book.

607.   The film was directed by Henry Selick. Selick also directed The Nightmare Before Christmas.

Corpse Bride
2005

608.   The stop-motion was so painstaking for this film, the animators used to have nightmares about it.

609.   It took 55 weeks to shoot all of the stop-motion.

610.   The tagline was, "The love of her afterlife."

611.   The puppets were made of stainless steel and then covered in silicone skin.

612.   The conclusion revolves around a character drinking poisoned wine. This idea was taken from the ending of Hamlet.

613.   Johnny Depp voices Victor. Deep Roy voices Bonesapart. Helena Bonham Carter voices the Corpse Bride. Christopher Lee voices Galswells. All these actors starred in Charlie and the Chocolate Factory.

The Croods
2013

614.   Nicholas Cage was offered the titular role in Shrek but he turned it down. He said it was the biggest regret of his career and he shouldn't have underestimated an animated film. When he was offered the role of Grug in this film, he accepted.

615.   The original title was Crood's Awakening.

616.   The story was supposed to be a buddy comedy between Guy and Grug.

617.   The film stars many actors who have appeared in Marvel movies including Nicholas Cage (Ghost Rider,) Emma Stone, (Gwen Stacy in Amazing Spider-Man,) and Ryan Reynolds (Deadpool.)

618.   Almost none of the animals in the film ever existed. Most of the creatures are chimaeras; a fusion of multiple animals put together.

619.   It took eight years to make the film.

620.   The tagline is "Meet the first modern family."

621.   The Croods have no idea what the outside world is like because Grug won't let them leave the cave.
         This idea is based on a concept called Plato's Cave. The Greek philosopher, Plato, described a scenario where a group of people are chained to a cave wall. There is a fire behind them which projects shadows onto the wall in front of the chained men. If something passes the fire e.g. a fly, a bird, a rat, etc. its shadow will be projected on the wall.
         Since this is all the men can see, this is the only reality the men are aware of. Because of this, the men would have no desire to leave the cave because they are unaware of a world beyond it.

Despicable Me
2010

622.   The Minions don't speak in gibberish. Everything they say translates into actual words.

623.   The story of Sleeping Kittens is an actual book.

624.   The director does the voice of the Minions.

625.   Felonius Gru says that Miss Hattie's face is "como un burro." This is Spanish for "like a donkey."

626.   The Minions were created to make Gru more likable.

627.   Steve Carell based his voice as Gru on Bela Lugosi (Dracula) and Ricardo Montalban (Khan from Star Trek II.)

628.   Gru's appearance is based on an Emperor penguin. This is fitting as the Emperor penguin is the only penguin species where the male looks after the young.

629.   Mr. Perkins' design is based on The Boss from the comic strip and cartoon, Dilbert.

630.   Mr. Perkins is voiced by Will Arnett. He put on weight for the role because he thought it would help to voice the heavy-set character.

631.   Julie Andrews voices Gru's mother.

632.   In the original script, Gru was much eviller. He wore bunny slippers made of actual bunnies and used a toothbrush made of human teeth. He was also supposed to have a room full of brains in his house.

633.   Originally, Gru looked dramatically different. He wore a gown with a skull on the front. He had hair and was very tall and gaunt.

634.   Russel Brand voices Dr. Nefario.

635.   "Gru" is French for "crane."

636.   Gru's walk is based on Mr. Bean and Charlie Chaplin.

637.   The original title was Evil Me.

638.   The Bank of Evil has the subtitle "Formerly Lehman Brothers" over the door.

639.   Kyle is a hybrid of a pit bull and a piranha.

640.   Dr. Nefario is 150 years old.

641.   The budget was $69 million. It grossed $543 million at the box office.

642.   The tagline is "Superbad. Superdad."

643.   In one draft, Gru fought a superhero called Hindsight.

644.   The DVD came with three Minion Shorts; Banana, Home Makeover, and Orientation Day.

645.   The Minions were meant to look like normal henchmen but the studio didn't have enough money so their design was made simpler.

Despicable Me 2
2013

646. Al Pacino was originally cast as the villain, Eduardo. Although he recorded all his lines, he dropped out after having a disagreement with the director. He was replaced with Benjamin Bratt.

647. Eduardo calls Gru "cabeza de huevo." This translates into "egg head."

648. One of Gru's quick-dial buttons is for Mom.

649. The poster contains over 10,400 Minions.

650. The budget was $76 million. It grossed over $970 million at the box office.

651. To promote the film, Steve Carell appeared on the show, Ellen, dressed as Gru.

652. Kristen Wiig voices Lucy. She voices Miss Hattie in the first film.

653. When the Minions mutate, they turn purple. This colour was chosen because it is on the opposite side of the spectrum to yellow.

654. The mutating Minion idea was inspired by Looney Tunes episode where Tweety mutates into a monster and terrorises Sylvester.

655. The tagline is "When the world needed a hero, they called a villain."

656. The DVD had three shorts; Panic in the Mailroom, Puppy Have You Seen Them?, and Training Wheels.

657. When the ice cream truck appears, the Minions shout "gelato," which is Italian for "ice cream."

Despicable Me 3
2017

658.   Trey Parker voices the villain, Balthazar Bratt. Trey
Parker created South Park with Matt Stone and voices Cartman
on the show.   Balthazar's robot resembles the children
characters from that show.

659.   John Cena was considered for the role of Balthazar.

660.   Balthazar Bratt's name is a reference to Benjamin Bratt,
who voiced the villain in the previous film.

661.   The tagline was, "Oh, brother."

662.   One of the prisoners has the same teddy bear as Mr. Bean.

663.   The Grinch appears on Margo's shirt. This is a reference to
the studio's next film.

664.   Parts of Balthazar's lair are based on the Neon Mix Tape
level in Plants vs Zombies 2.

665.   The film cost $80 million. It made over $1 billion dollars
at the box office. It was the only film released in the summer of
2017 to make a billion dollars.

666.   Gru was born in the fictional European country,
Freedonia. This is the same name of the country that appears in
The Marx Brothers film, Duck Soup.

667.   The diamond in the trailer is a parody of the Pink Panther
diamond.

668.   The film was shipped to cinemas under the name, Double
Bubble.

Dumbo
1941

669.   This was the first animated Disney film set in modern day. It was also the first Disney film to be set in America and to be released on video cassette.

670.   Dumbo is friends with Timothy Mouse. Timothy was supposed to be a robin.

671.   Timothy's name is unknown until the very end.

672.   Originally, the film was going to be a 30-minute short.

673.   The film won an Oscar for Best Music.

674.   This is John Lasseter's favourite film. He has directed at least five Pixar films including Toy Story.

675.   The film cost $950,000. It made $1.6 million upon its originally run. Although it was the fourth Disney film, it was the second to make a profit.

676.   During the making of this film, half of the animators went on strike. Their likeness was used for the clowns that "hit the big boss for a raise."

677.   There was supposed to be a sequel in 2000 but production never got further than storyboarding.

678.   The film's concept is similar to the story of Red Nosed Reindeer. Both stories revolve around a character being mocked because of a physical deformity (Rudolf's nose and Dumbo's big ears.)
        Eventually the main character uses this deformity to become popular (Rudolf's bright nose leads the sleigh so Santa can see where he's going and Dumbo becomes famous when he learns to fly with his ears.)

679.   Verna Felton voices Jumbo and the Elephant Matriarch. She voices many iconic Disney roles such as the Fairy Godmother in Cinderella, Aunt Sarah in Lady and the Tramp, the

Queen of Hearts in Alice in Wonderland, and Flora in Sleeping Beauty.

680.   Dumbo is the first protagonist in a Disney film to have no dialogue.

681.   The film is only 64 minutes long. Walt Disney's distributor didn't want to release the film as a major motion picture because it was too short.

682.   The only thing that Jumbo says is Dumbo's real name, Jumbo Jr.

683.   Although many people find the crows to be offensive for depicting African American stereotypes, the studio pointed out that they are among the only friendly and intelligent characters in the film. Also, most of the crows are voiced by black actors in a time where African-Americans struggled to get acting work.

        The problem with this argument is that the crow leader, Jim, is voiced by a white actor.

Early Man
2018

684.   The film was produced by Aardman Animation, who are best-known for creating Wallace and Gromit. Wallace and Gromit cameo in one of the crowd shots. The director didn't realise the animators did this until post-production.

685.   The original title was Early Man-United.

686.   The tagline was, "Invent soccer. Make prehistory."

687.   Tom Hiddleston provides the voice of Lord Nooth. He was cast after the director saw Hiddleston perform his Robert De Niro impression on The Graham Norton Show.

688.   Timothy Spall provides the voice of Chief Bobnar. This is the second Aardman film he has been a part of since Spall starred in Chicken Run.

689.   The Beady Eyed Penguin from the Wallace and Gromit short, The Wrong Trousers, appears on a cave wall in the end credits.

690.   Four of the actors have appeared in Harry Potter films.

691.   The bit where Dug, Goona, and Hognob fall out of a window and land on a roll of toilet roll was supposed to be in the Aardman film, The Curse of the Were-Rabbit, but the director couldn't figure out a way to incorporate it into the story. He had to wait 13 years to put this gag in a film.

The Emoji Movie
2017

692.   TJ Miller voices the lead character, Gene the Meh Emoji. He claims that this is the fastest produced animated film ever.

693.   The original title was Emojimovie: Express Yourself.

694.   The teaser trailer was met with so much hate, the production hoped they could get people interested in the movie by casting a big star. Only months before the film was released, Patrick Stewart was cast as Poop. This is why Poop is voiced by a different actor in the original trailer.

695.   The tagline was, "Welcome to the secret world inside your phone."

696.   The film was torn apart by critics and is considered to be one of the worst animated films ever. Despite the fact the movie was universally panned, The Emoji Movie made a profit because many people were curious to see how bad it was.

697.   Patrick Stewart provides the voice of Poop. Originally, Jordan Peele was offered the role. He was so offended that he considered quitted acting.

The Emperor's New Groove
2000

698.   Renowned playwright, David Mamet, said the film's script was one of the most brilliantly innovative things Hollywood has produced in years.

699.   Although the film tanked at the box office, it is now considered to be one of the most underrated Disney films. It is ranked higher on Rotten Tomatoes than some Disney classics like Alice in Wonderland and Peter Pan.

700.   The original title was Kingdom of the Sun.

701.   Kuzco is named after the Inca capital, Cuzco.

702.   John Goodman voices Pacha. "Pacha" is Incan for "Earth."

703.   Disney saw the story as a Peruvian version of The Prince and the Pauper.

704.   The tagline is "Llama llama ding dong."

705.   Some people assumed that the title is referencing Hans Christian Anderson's story, The Emperor's New Clothes. The two stories are not connected.

706.   In the diner, the saltshakers are shaped like llamas.

707.   Eartha Kitt voices Yzma. Barbara Streisand was considered for Yzma.

708.   Yzma turns into a cat at the end of the film. This is a reference to Eartha Kitt's most iconic role, Catwoman in the 1966 TV series, Batman.

709.   Patrick Warburton voices Kronk. He is best-known for voicing Joe in Family Guy.

710.   The sequel, Kronk's New Groove, was released in 2005. It received a score of 0% on Rotten Tomatoes.

711.   The squirrel is called Plucky.

712.   Pacha's wife, Chicha, is pregnant. This is the first Disney film to show a pregnant character.

713.   Sting sang two of the songs in the film. When Disney offered him the job, he said he would only agree to it if his wife was given unlimited access to make a documentary about the documentary. The doc is called The Sweatbox.

714.   When Disney execs saw a rough cut of the film, they demanded the script to be rewritten. Sting was devastated because he spent two years writing the music for the film. He was so upset, he packed up everything and went to the Himalayas to destress.

715.   All but two of Sting's songs were cut because Disney believed the musician's voice sounded too old. They replaced most of his songs with music from Tom Jones...who is 11 years older than Sting.

716.   The film concludes with Cuzco building a waterslide. This made Sting so angry, he said he wanted "vengeance" upon Disney. He wrote a letter to the execs reading, "Gentlemen, when you have achieved genuine human values, you don't need a theme park or a water slide."

Fantasia
1940

717.   The original title was Colours and Music.

718.   The sorcerer is called Yensid. His facial expressions are based on Walt Disney. Also, his name is "Disney" backwards.

719.   Yensid's appearance was used again for the King of Atlantis in the Disney film, Atlantis: The Lost Empire.

720.   Fantasia is 125 minutes, making it the longest animated Disney film ever.

721.   This is the first Disney feature film that Mickey Mouse appears in.

722.   Visionary painter, Salvador Dali, painted some work for the film but it wasn't used.

723.   James Cagney, Cecil B. DeMille, and Shirley Temple attended the premier.

724.   The beast in the final scene is not the Devil. It's a Slavic demon called Czernobog.

725.   Bela Lugosi modelled for the demon, Czernobog. Bela Lugosi is famous for playing Dracula.

726.   The film cost $2.3 million.

727.   There are over 500 characters in Fantasia.

728.   This was Disney's third feature film.

729.   Mickey Mouse is the star of the film. Originally, it was going to be Dopey from Snow White and the Seven Dwarfs.

730.   Walt Disney intended to rerelease the film every year with different music.

731.   This is Steven Spielberg's favourite animated movie.

732.   Over a thousand artists and technicians made the film.

733.   Walt Disney strongly considered using different scents to maximise the experience. He intended to spray jasmine for the Waltz of the Flowers section, incense for Ave Maria, and gunpowder for The Sorcerer's Apprentice. The idea was dropped because it was too complicated.

734.   This was the first film to depict a stegosaurus using its clubbed tail as a weapon.

735.   The tagline is "Where every sound creates a picture."

736.   Wilfred Jackson directed Snow White and the Seven Dwarfs, Cinderella, Fantasia, Dumbo, Peter Pan, and Pinocchio. He also pioneered the synching of animation, sound, and the blending of animation with live-action. Despite the fact that the world of animation owes so much to him, his name is mostly forgotten.

737.   Disney studios still get complaints that the final scene is too scary.

Fantasia 2000
1999

738.   It took nine years to make this film.

739.   The film had many iconic hosts including Bette Midler, James Earl Jones, Angela Lansbury, Steve Martin, and Penn & Teller.

740.   This is the first animated film presented in IMAX.

741.   It was originally called Fantasia Continued.

742.   The Disney chairman, Jeffrey Katzenberg, thought making a sequel to Fantasia was a bad idea. Because of this, Fantasia 2000 was made without his knowledge or involvement.

743.   Walt Disney believed Fantasia was a failure because it came out during World War II and wasn't released in Europe.
        Over the years, it was perceived as a masterpiece so Walt knew it should have a sequel. Although Disney studios put $80 million into this movie, it barely broke even, only making $91 million at the box office.

744.   Because Disney studios assumed Fantasia 2000 would be a success, they worked on several shorts for another sequel. These shorts were called Destino, Lorenzo, One by One, and The Little Matchgirl.
        Since a third Fantasia film was abandoned, these shorts were released separately between 2003 and 2006.

Fantastic Mr. Fox
2009

745.   The story is based on the Roald Dahl's book that was written in 1970.

746.   Just before Dahl wrote the book, one of his children died from measles and another one of his children suffered water on the brain. This encouraged Dahl to write a book where the father character is the protector of his family.

747.   Bean's appearance is based on Roald Dahl.

748.   Meryl Streep voices Mrs. Felicity Fox. She was named after Roald Dahl's wife.

749.   The flooding of the mine was the only scene where CGI was used. Every other shot was created with stop-motion.

750.   535 puppets were made for the film. 102 were made for the titular character.

751.   The tagline is "Dig the life fantastic."

752.   The colour scheme is mostly made of autumn-related colours like yellow, orange, and brown. There is very little green and blue in the entire film.

753.   To make the characters look realistic, the director used real animal fur.

754.   It took seven months to make the first puppet of Mr. Fox.

755.   Mr. Fox bears his teeth when frightened. Foxes do this in real life.

756.   Only the first hour is based on Roald Dahl's book.

757.   The human's hair is made of real human hair.

758.   Wes Anderson directed the film. Fantastic Mr. Fox was the first book he ever owned.

759.   The director cameos as Weasel.

760.   Wes Anderson directed most of the film via email and barely spent any time on set.

761.   Mr. Fox's suits are based on Wes Anderson's own clothing.

762.   Sometimes, Wes recorded himself acting out a scene and then sent it to the animators to show them how he wanted the characters to move.

763.   Wes Anderson had the actors record their lines outside. One of the takes was nearly ruined by a boat passing by. The director manipulated the sound so it sounded like a passing plane and incorporated it into the scene.

Ferdinand
2017

764. The film is based on The Story of Ferdinand, which was written by Munro Leaf in 1936. During World War II, it was banned in Italy, Germany and Russia for being "too nice."

765. Una, Dos, and Quatro's spinning motion is based on Sonic the Hedgehog's spinball attack in the Sonic video game series.

766. John Cena voices Ferdinand. This is the fourth animated film he has worked on.

767. Kate McKinnon voices Lupe. This is the third animated film she has worked on since she starred in The Angry Birds Movie and Finding Dory.

768. Ferdinand lives in Ronda in the south of Spain. This village has the world's oldest bull-ring. It was built in 1785.

769. This is the fourth film that Blue Sky Studios have made that is based on a book. The other films were Horton Hears a Who!, Epic, and The Peanuts Movie.

770. The film spawned a mobile game called Ferdinand: Unstoppabull.

771. The film was meant to be released in July 2017 but it was delayed so it wouldn't have to compete with summer blockbusters. Ironically, it came out the same day as Star Wars: The Last Jedi.

772. At one point, Angus says, "I'm a bull, not a doctor." It refers to the famous line, "I'm a doctor, not a mechanic," that Dr Bones McCoy says throughout Star Trek.

773. This is the sixth animated film that Carolos Saldanha has directed. He directed Ice Age, Ice Age 2, Ice Age 3, Rio, Rio 2, and Robots.

774. Disney made a short called Ferdinand the Bull in 1938.

Ferngully: The Last Rainforest
1992

775.   This was the first animated film that Robin Williams starred in. He voices Batty Koda.

776.   The tagline was, "Do you believe in humans?"

777.   Ferngully is based on the rainforest of Australia.

778.   The film was directed by Bill Kroyer. This is the only film he ever made.

779.   Elton John performed the song, Some Other World. It was the first time he worked on an animated film.

780.   Many people complain that the film, Avatar, copied the story of Ferngully.

781.   The film's message is to protect the rainforest. Many critics pointed out the irony of making an animated film with this message since thousands of trees had to be cut down to make the paper for the animation.

Final Fantasy VII: Advent Children
2005

782.   Mena Suvari voices Aerith. She is best-known for playing Angela in American Beauty and Heather in American Pie.

783.   Cloud uses five Limit Breaks in the film.

784.   The final battle had to be re-animated as it was considered too gory.

785.   Loz's ring tone is the Final Fantasy Victory music.

786.   When Loz fights Tifa, the background music is the Battle theme from the video game series.

787.   In the original trailer, all the characters looked Asian. In this film, all the characters look more anime-like.

788.   The tagline is "I won't just be a memory."

789.   Kadaj calls upon the dragon, Bahamut. In Final Fantasy VII, there are three versions of this dragon; Bahamut, Neo Bahamut, and Bahamut Zero. The dragon in the film is called Bahamut Sin.

790.   Vincent's three-barrelled gun is called Cerberus. It is named after the three-headed dog that guards the gates of Tartarus in Greek mythology.

791.   Cloud's bike is called Fenrir. It is named after a monstrous wolf in Norse mythology.

Final Fantasy: The Spirits Within
2001

792.   There's an extra on the DVD that shows the main characters performing Michael Jackson's thriller.

793.   Ming-Na Wen voices the lead character, Aki. She also voices the titular character in the Disney film, Mulan.

794.   Donald Sutherland voices Sid. There's a character called Sid in almost every Final Fantasy game.

795.   The film cost $137 million. It only made $85 million at the box office, making it one of the most unsuccessful films ever at the time.
    Despite the fact the film was a flop, it had the highest rating of any movie based on a video game according to Rotten Tomatoes at the time.

796.   The story takes place in 2065.

797.   Although most characters and objects were computer-generated, the backgrounds were hand painted.

798.   The film took four years to make. As the animators were finishing the last few shots, they had to fix some of the earliest shots because they looked so dated by comparison.

799.   The animators spent 20% of their time making sure Aki's hair looked right.

800.   Ving Rhames voices Ryan. Originally, Ryan was going to have a cybernetic arm. This is a reference to Barrett from Final Fantasy VII who had a robotic arm.

801.   Matt McKenzie voices the Major. He voices Auron in Final Fantasy X. He is the only actor to voice a character in this film and the video game series.

Finding Nemo
2003

802.   Nemo first appeared as a toy in Boo's room in Monsters, Inc.

803.   Pixar made the water look so realistic that they had to make it look LESS realistic in case audience members thought it was real footage of the ocean.

804.   Finding Nemo is the most successful DVD of all time. It sold 41 million copies.

805.   Crush says "dude" 21 times.

806.   This was the first Pixar film to win an Oscar for Best Animated Feature.

807.   Because Marlin and Dory have opposite personalities, their colours are inverted. Marlin is orange and white. Dory is black and blue.

808.   The Disney CEO at the time, Michael Eisner, was certain the film would fail.

809.   William H. Macy was originally cast as Marlin. Although he recorded all his lines, Pixar believed his voice wasn't right and so, replaced him with Albert Brooks.

810.   Albert Brooks' real name is Albert Einstein. Seriously.

811.   Albert Brooks didn't like making the film as he found recording his lines exhausting.

812.   The animators studied dog eyes to animate expressions on the fish.

813.   This was the first Pixar film to show blood.

814.   This was the second most successful film of 2003. The most successful film of the year was The Lord of the Rings: Return of the King.

815.   It took Albert Brooks a day to record the scene where Marlin tells a joke.

816.   Buzz Lightyear appears on the floor of the waiting room.

817.   The mermaid in the aquarium tank was in the short film, Knick Knack. Knick Knack was one of the first shorts Pixar ever created in 1989.

818.   Pixar started working on the film in 1997. It wasn't released until 2003.

819.   Mike from Monsters, Inc. appears in the closing credits.

820.   The director, Andrew Stanton, voices Crush the turtle and the seagulls that say, "Mine!" He lay down on his couch while recording his lines as Crush to sound as relaxed as possible.

821.   Stanton was making this film the same time he was making A Bug's Life.

822.   200 turtles were animated for Crush's scene.

823.   Nicholas Bird voices Crush's son, Squirt. He is the son of Brad Bird. Bird directed Ratatouille and The Incredibles.

824.   The turtles' shells are designed to look like Hawaiian shirts.

825.   The girl with the braces is called Darla. The music that plays when she is present is based on the iconic Psycho theme song.

826.   This is the first Pixar film to have a post-credits scene.

827.   There's a kid in the dentist waiting room that's reading a comic book with Mr. Incredible on the back cover. The Incredibles didn't come out for another year.

828.   Dory keeps getting Nemo's name wrong. She calls him Chico, Elmo, Harpo, Bingo, and Fabio.

829.   The dentist is called Dr. Philip Sherman. He has an award certificates in his office for "Gums Most Likely to Recede Award" and "The Toothless Grin Award."

830.   The scene where the seagulls are staring ominously at Marlin and Dory is based on Hitchcock's film, The Birds.

831.   Ellen DeGeneres got cast as Dory after the Pixar studio watched her on her show and noticed that she changed the subject every five seconds. This suits the character of Dory since she suffers from short-term memory loss.

832.   The dentist has a deep fryer in his office.

833.   John Ratzenberger voices the Fish School. Ratzenberger has appeared in more Pixar films than any other actor.

834.   When Gill explains his escape plan, you can see the Pizza Planet truck from Toy Story.

835.   To make the underwater scenes look as realistic as possible, some of the crewmembers had to make recordings of the Great Barrier Reef. Each of these filmmakers had to receive a SCUBA certificate to enter the Reef.

836.   When the filmmakers were about to film the scene where Marlin tells Dory to go home, there was only ten minutes left before the studio closed for the night. The crew assumed Ellen DeGeneres would struggle with an emotional scene since her background was mainly in comedy. They asked her to do a test recording and they would try and get it right the following day. The first recording was so perfect, it was used for the final cut.

837.   The great white shark is called Bruce. Bruce is the name of the shark in Jaws. It was named after the director's lawyer.

838.   The sound used for Nemo's bad fin was taken from scrunching a paper towel.

839.   One of the writers spent hours talking to a dentist to make sure the tools at the dentistry were as accurate as possible.

840.   Dory is a Regal Blue Tang fish. Marlin is a clownfish. The success of this film led to Tang fish and clownfish becoming popular pets. Sadly, both fish are very difficult to look after and many pet owners accidentally killed them.

Some pet owners took the "setting fish free" concept too literally. Many children chucked their fish down the toilet, believing it would lead them to the sea. These fish died before they reached the sewer.

Some pet owners bought clownfish just so they could release them in the sea, not knowing that the species is venomous, which decimated the ecology in certain areas, especially in Florida.

Also, the demand for clownfish was so high, the fisherman struggled to find them. In certain areas, the clownfish population dropped by 75%.

841.   It took the animators four days to work on one frame of the underwater scenes. One frame of footage makes up $1/24^{th}$ of a second.

842.   The animators studied how light passes through gummy bears to understand how light passes through fish.

843.   At the end of the film, the fish escape from a net by swimming downward, breaking free from the attached ship. The weirdest thing about this scene is that it is based on a real incident. In Norway, a group of fish capsized a ship by swimming down while trapped in the ship's net.

844.   Nemo plans to escape from a fish tank by damaging the filter. The filmmakers' dismantled the biofiltration unit of a fish tank to make sure this concept was plausible.

845.   Dory's short-term memory loss is a reference to the misconception that goldfish have a three-second memory. In reality, goldfish can remember things for up to a month.

846.   Originally, the audience wouldn't know why Marlin was so protective of Nemo for most the movie. This was changed as it made Marlin come across as annoying and unsympathetic.

847.   In real life, clownfish are hermaphrodites.

848.   Willem Dafoe voices Gill. The scars on Gill's face is based on the creases on Dafoe's face.

849.   Gill was originally going to be Marlin's sidekick instead of Dory.

850.   Although Marlin's species is often known as a clownfish, its biological name is an anemonefish.

851.   The boats at the dock are called Major Plot Point, For the Birds, Skiff-A-Dee-Do-Dah, Sea Monkey, Peer Pressure, Bow Movement, Knottie Buoy, The Surly Mermaid, and iBoat.

852.   The film cost $94 million. It grossed $940 million at the box office, making it the first animated film to be more successful than The Lion King. When the producer of The Lion King heard this, he said, "It's about time."

853.   Gill's eclectic group in the fish tank are based on the characters in the film, One Flew Over the Cuckoo's Nest.

854.   Nemo's name is a reference to Captain Nemo in Jules Verne's novel, 20,000 Leagues Under the Sea. It means "nobody" in Latin.

855.   There was supposed to be a scene where the sharks are playing volleyball with sea mines.

856.   The seagulls are modelled after the penguin from the Wallace and Gromit short, The Wrong Trousers.

857.   The tagline is, "71% of the Earth's surface is covered by water. That's a lot of space to find one fish."

858.   This is the first Pixar film that doesn't take place in the United States.

859.   The director, Andrew Stanton, pitched the idea to Pixar in an hour-long presentation. When he finished, the head of Pixar said, "You had me at fish."

Finding Dory
2016

860.   Idris Elba and Dominic West voice the sea lions, Fluke and Rudder. Both actors starred in The Wire.

861.   The story was supposed to take place in an aquatic park but Pixar decided not to after the controversy from the documentary, Blackfish.

862.   Ed O' Neill voices Hank. Ty Burrell voices Bailey. Both actors star in Modern Family.

863.   The tagline is, "She just kept swimming."

864.   The director cast many actors by watching The Ellen DeGeneres Show and observed who had the best chemistry with Ellen. This is how Diane Keaton, Ed O' Neill, and Ty Burrell were cast.

865.   Technically, Hank is not an octopus because he only has seven tentacles, which makes him a septopus. The animators couldn't animate him properly with eight tentacles so they removed one.

866.   The animators wanted Hank to look anatomically correct so they placed his beak under his tentacles. In most animation, an octopus' mouth is placed below its eyes. Because Hank's beak couldn't be seen when he talked, the animators had to make his eyes more expressive so the audience could understand how he felt.

867.   Ellen DeGeneres voices the titular character. The film was first announced by DeGeneres on her show.

868.   The film is set a year after Finding Nemo.

869.   Hank has 350 suction cups on his tentacles.

870.   Kaitlin Olson voices Destiny. Olson is best-known for playing Dee in It's Always Sunny in Philadelphia.

871.   Riley from Inside Out can be seen for a second after Dory falls into Destiny's tank.

872.   Hank the septopus can camouflage himself. As an April Fool's joke, the director announced that Hank had appeared in every single Pixar film but no one noticed because he was camouflaged.

873.   The first scene with Hank was so difficult to animate, the animators created 146 versions of it and let the director pick the scene he liked the best.

874.   John Ratzenberger voices Bill the Crab. He is starred in more Pixar films than any other actor.

875.   The short, Piper, was shown before this film during its theatrical release.

876.   Weirdly, Hank had to be made less charismatic because the test audiences found him so entertaining, it was pulling focus away from Dory.

877.   It was very difficult to animate Hank because he has no bones. Because of this, the animators found it very difficult to create a blueprint of Hank. It took over a year to make Hank's movements look right.

878.   Hanks' movements are based on Kaa from The Jungle Book.

879.   The film cost $200 million. The film made over a billion dollars.

880.   The writers found it so hard to tell the story of a character who suffers from memory problems, they strongly considered "fixing" Dory's memory. They eventually decided not to do this as Dory's amnesia is a fundamental part of her character.

Flushed Away
2006

881.   Flushed Away was made by Aardman studios; the same studio that makes the Wallace and Gromit animations.

882.   This was the first CGI-film that Aardman made.

883.   In one scene, Hugh Jackman's character, Roddy, pulls out a Wolverine outfit from a wardrobe. Hugh Jackman portrays Wolverine in the X-Men films.

884.   At the start of the film, one of the outfits that Roddy pulls out of the wardrobe belongs to Wallace from Wallace and Gromit.

885.   Kate Winslet voices Rita. Nicole Kidman was considered for the role.

886.   One of the frozen rats in the fridge is Han Solo from Star Wars.

887.   Jean Reno voices Le Frog. Johnny Depp and Kevin Kline were considered for the role.

888.   A picture of Shrek appears on the fridge.

889.   The tagline is "Plumbing soon."

890.   When Roddy gets flushed, an orange fish shouts, "Have you seen my dad?" This is a reference to Finding Nemo.

891.   The Toad wears a Freemason ring.

892.   Andy Serkis voices Spike. Robert De Niro auditioned for the role.

Foodfight!
2012

893.   This is considered to be the worst 3D animated film ever.

894.   The story revolves around food products coming to life when there are no humans around. (Basically, it's Toy Story with food.) Many food brands were supposed to appear like Count Chocula and Chester Cheetah but they pulled out, believing the film would fail at the box office.

895.   The film was directed by Lawrence Kasanoff. He tried to make a Tetris film but his story was so complex, he believed it could only work as a trilogy. He is still working on it.

896.   The director was certain this film would be a hit and claimed his company was "the new Pixar." The film cost $65 million. It only made $73,706 at the box office. This means that it made slightly more than 0.1% of its budget back.

897.   If the film was successful, the director was going to create an event called Foodfight on Ice, similar to Disney on Ice.

898.   The film was supposed to come out in 2003. It was delayed for nine years. The reason why Foodfight! was so heavily delayed is because the hard drive containing key footage was stolen. This means that the animators lost years of work and had to start all over again.

899.   According to the animators, the director didn't understand the difference between live-action and animation. He asked the crew to do "retakes" of the scenes and told the animators to make the scenes "more awesome" and "30% better." The director was fired due to his incompetence and the studio had to finish the remainder of the film.

900.   Many animators who worked on the film don't mention it on their resumes.

The Fox and the Hound
1981

901.   The fox is called Tod. Tod is derived from the Middle English word "todde" which means "fox."

902.   The tagline is "Two friends that didn't know they were supposed to be enemies."

903.   The film was delayed for a year as many animators left to join Disney's competitor, Don Bluth.

904.   The story is based on Daniel P. Mannix's novel of the same. The film has very little resemblance to the novel.

905.   Kurt Russell voices Copper. Corey Feldman voices Young Copper.

906.   Renowned director, Tim Burton, animated the character, Vixey.

907.   Mickey Rooney voices Tod.

908.   The sequel, The Fox and the Hound 2, was released in 2006.

909.   The bear's roar is the same as Shere Kahn's roar in The Jungle Book.

Frankenweenie
2012

910.   The turtle is called Shelley. This is an obvious reference to the fact that turtles have shells. It is also a reference to the writer of Frankenstein, Mary Shelley, which was the main inspiration for this film.

911.   The mayor is called Burgermeister, which means "mayor" in German.

912.   Winona Ryder voices Elsa Van Helsing. Catherine O' Hara voices Mrs. Frankenstein. The two actresses worked on Tim Burton's film, Beetlejuice.

913.   Elsa Van Helsing's first name is a reference to Elsa Lanchester, who played the Bride in the Bride of Frankenstein. Her surname is based on Abraham Van Helsing. He battled Dracula in Bram Stoker's novel, Dracula.

914.   This film is a remake of the 30-minute short that Tim Burton made in 1984.

915.   Martin Landau voices Mr. Rzykruski. Rzykruski's appearance is based on Vincent Price. Price played the Inventor in Tim Burton's film, Edward Scissorhands.

916.   E. Gore's name is a reference to Ygor from the film, Son of Frankenstein.

917.   If the film wasn't allowed to be in black-and-white, Tim Burton wouldn't have made it.

918.   Zero's grave can be seen in the pet cemetery. Zero was the name of the dog in The Nightmare Before Christmas.

919.   Shelley the tortoise becomes a gigantic monster. This is a reference to the film, Gamera, which revolves around a colossal tortoise-like creature.

920.   One of the graves in the pet cemetery reads "Goodbye Kitty." It resembles the Hello Kitty logo.

921.   Burton made the 1984 version of Frankenweenie when he worked for Disney. Disney considered the film to be too scary for children and had Burton fired.

922.   Elsa's dog is called Persephone. Persephone was the wife of Hades in Greek mythology.

923.   Persephone has a white streak in her hair, just like the Bride in Bride of Frankenstein.

Frozen
2013

924.   The short, Get a Horse!, was shown in the cinema before this film.

925.   Elsa is 21. Anna is 18. Hans is 23.

926.   Flights from the US to Norway tripled immediately after Frozen came out as many Americans wanted to visit the same landscapes that inspired the film.

927.   The film is based on Hans Christian Anderson's story, The Snow Queen.

928.   Hans Christian Anderson's name is referenced in four of the character's names – Hans, Kristoff, Anna, and Sven.

929.   This is the first Disney film that succeeds at the Bechdel test. The Bechdel test represents whether a work of fiction has two female characters that talk to each other about something other than a man.
    Many franchises fail at this test including the original Star Wars trilogy, The Lord of the Rings films, and all but one of the Harry Potter movies.

930.   Elsa was supposed to turn into the villain when she fled from the village. After executives heard the song, Let It Go, they changed their mind. As a villain, Elsa had blue hair and wore a dress made of weasels.

931.   A woman tried to sue Disney because she believed that Frozen was a retelling of her 2010 biography. Some of the similarities she pointed out included "intense sisterly love," "two male characters," and "recluse sister."

932.   Originally, Anna and Elsa weren't related.

933.   Josh Gad voices Olaf. He improvised a lot of his dialogue.

934.   The story takes place in the 1840s. Originally, it was going to take place in the 1700s.

935.   The characters wear Norwegian clothing. Originally, they were going to wear Russian garments.

936.   The film cost $150 million. It made $1,276,480,335, making it the most successful animated film at the time.

937.   Gad took his daughter to the cinema to see Monsters University when she was four years old. Before the film started, there was a trailer for Frozen that shows Olaf laughing. Gad's daughter instantly recognised her father's laugh and said "That's Dada, more Dada." Gad immediately started crying.

938.   Elsa's castle was animated by 50 people.

939.   A live reindeer was brought into the studio so the animators could make Sven look more realistic.

940.   Kerry Wilson filed a lawsuit against Disney as she believed the teaser trailer for Frozen was based on her 2014 short film, The Snowman.

941.   Rapunzel and Flynn can be seen when the gates open during the "For the First Time in Forever" song.

942.   The United States suffered the coldest winter in years the same year this film was released. Many Americans joked that Elsa was responsible.

943.   Although the two main characters are female, less than 50% of the dialogue is spoken by female characters.

944.   The film has a post-credits scene.

945.   Elsa is the second Disney princess to become a Queen. The first was Kida in Atlantis: The Lost Empire.

946.   Jack Whitehall voiced one of the trolls but his dialogue was cut.

947.   Idina Menzel voices Elsa. This is the third time she has collaborated with Disney. She voices the sorceress, Circe, in the

animated series, Hercules, and she played Nancy in the film, Enchanted.

948.   Kristen Bell voices Anna. Her daughters don't like the film.

949.   Kristen Bell has a habit of biting her lip. This was incorporated into the character.

950.   Han's horse is called Sitron. "Sitron" is Norwegian for "lemon."

951.   Elsa has 420,000 strands of hair which is 15 times more hair than Rapunzel in Tangled.

952.   The animators had to wear dresses and run through snow to get a sense of how a dress moved in a blizzard. The animators were men.

953.   Hans mentions that he has 12 older brothers. This means that he is the 13th child, which implies his evil nature.

954.   Idina Menzel's son bragged that her mum sings the song, Let It Go. When he said this in school, one kid said, "So does everyone else."

955.   Let It Go has been recorded in at least 41 languages.

956.   Three million hours went into making this film over 2.5 years.

957.   The colours in Elsa's ice castle represent her feelings – blue represents happy, red represents fear, and yellow represents anger.

958.   Do You Want to Build a Snowman? was nearly cut.

959.   Sven was going to be called Thor.

960.   When the snow monster screams, its gesture and facial expressions are identical to when Sulley roars in Monsters, Inc..

961.   Olaf's name is a reference to "Oh laugh."

962.   The first and last thing that the King says is, "Elsa."

963.   This was the third most successful film of 2013. It was beaten by The Hunger Games: Catching Fire and Iron Man 3.

964.   Jennifer Lee directed Frozen. This was her directorial debut. She was the first woman to direct a Disney animated feature and to write the screenplay for an animated Disney film since Beauty and the Beast.
        Bizarrely, Jennifer Lee was never supposed to direct the film. Originally, she was the screenwriter.

965.   Elsa and Kristoff never speak to each other.

966.   A psychotherapist called Dr. Jill Squyres concluded that Elsa has Borderline Personality Disorder.

967.   It took nine months to animate Elsa's castle.

968.   600 people made this film.

969.   Anna's horse is called Kjekk. It means "handsome" in Norwegian.

970.   Anna is the only Disney princess to perform a duet with the villain.

971.   The film won two Oscars, two BAFTAs, and a Golden Globe.

972.   Elsa's original look was based on Amy Winehouse.

973.   In most films, good characters wear bright colours and villains wear dark colours. In this film, the villain wears the brightest clothing.

974.   In 2013, an animated film called The Legend of Sarila was released. The creators changed the title to Frozen Land when it was released in the US to capitalise on the success of Frozen.
        Even the font of the title was the same as Frozen and the main character was wearing the same colours as Anna. The filmmakers hoped consumers would think the movie was connected

to Frozen even though the story revolves around Eskimos and shamans.

Weirdly, Oscar-winning actor, Christopher Plummer, starred in this film.

975.   Walt Disney wanted to make this film in the 1940s.

976.   Ciaran Hinds voices Pabbie and Grandpa.

977.   Two of the guards are called Kai and Gerda. This is the name of two characters in the original story, The Snow Queen.

978.   The movie is 102 minutes long. Only 24 minutes is dedicated to the songs.

979.   Santino Fontana voices Hans. He originally auditioned for Kristoff.

980.   Santino Fontana sang I Feel Pretty for his audition.

981.   The giant snowman is called Marshmallow.

982.   Marshmallow was originally going to look like a gigantic version of Olaf.

983.   When Marshmallow throws Anna, she loses her hat. She has her hat back in the next scene.

984.   The movie was supposed to be in 2D.

985.   312 different faces were created for the characters in this film, which was more than any other animated Disney film at the time.

986.   The most complex frames in the movie were when Elsa walks onto the balcony of her castle. It took 132 hours to render each frame.

987.   Let It Go was written in one day by Robert Lopez. Lopez has also written music for the musicals, The Book of Mormon and Avenue Q.

988.   In this film, there is no explanation why Elsa can create ice. In the original script, one child is born with ice powers every millennium when the planets align with Saturn.

989.   The film spawned a short called Frozen Fever in 2015. It took six months to make this short.

990.   When Elsa sneezes in Frozen Fever, she creates mini-snowman called Snowgies. Baymax from Big Hero 6 cameos as one of the Snowgies.

991.   In the original script of Frozen Fever, Elsa created Olafs every time she sneezed. The writers decided not to do this as they didn't want to oversaturate the character.

992.   There is an Internet rumour that Elsa's parents didn't die at sea. Instead, they were washed up in Africa and were killed by a wild animal and their child grew up to be Tarzan.

Frozen II
2019

993.   Frozen II was meant to come out after the Disney film, Gigantic. After that film was scrapped, Frozen II's release date was pushed forward.

994.   This was the final Disney film that John Lasseter worked on. He is best-known for directing Toy Story, Toy Story 2, A Bug's Life, and Cars.

995.   The call used to lure Elsa to the enchanted forest is a Scandinavian herding technique called kulning.

996.   This is the first Disney princess sequel to be released in cinemas.

997.   A snow figurine of Dumbo can be seen in the opening scene when Elsa and Anna are playing in the forest.

998.   In Japan, the title is Anna and the Snow Queen 2. In Italy, the title is The Secret of Arendelle. In Norway, it's called Frost 2.

999.   The animators never rendered toes for Elsa in the previous film since the character has never barefooted. They had to completely remodel her feet for this movie.

1000.   Agnar mentions that he's reading a book by "some new Danish author." This is a reference to Hans Christian Anderson, who wrote The Snow Queen, which is the inspiration for Frozen.

1001.   In the conclusion of Frozen, Elsa gives Olaf a snow cloud to prevent him from melting. In the short, Olaf's Frozen Adventure, there was meant to be a song explaining that Elsa's magic had magnified, allowing her to make Olaf unmeltable.

The only reference to this in Frozen II is when Anna asks Olaf, "enjoying the new permafrost?"

1002.   Olaf says that turtles can breathe out of their butts. This is true. No, really. It is.

1003.   The salamander represents fire. In Ancient Greek times, people genuinely believed salamanders could produce fire by walking.

1004.   When Kristoff is singing Lost in the Woods, the three reindeer form a triangular formation. They are in the same pose as Queen for the cover of their album, Bohemian Rhapsody.

1005.   Young Elsa is voiced by Mattea Conforti. She played Young Anna in the Broadway adaptation of Frozen.

1006.   Josh Gad, who reprises the role of Olaf, improvised the lines about Samantha.

1007.   The story is set three years after the original film.

1008.   The film cost $150 million.

1009.   Baymax from Big Hero 6 appears as one of Anna's ice toys.

Fun & Fancy Free
1947

1010.   This was the first film that Mickey Mouse appeared in since Fantasia.

1011.   A portion of the film revolves around the Jack and the Beanstalk story. Billy Gilbert voices Willie the Giant. Gilbert also voices Sneezy in Snow White and the Seven Dwarfs.

1012.   This was the first film to credit the voice actor for Mickey Mouse. He was voiced by some guy called Walt Disney.

1013.   It took seven years to complete the film. The reason why it took so long was because the American military forced Disney's studio to make propaganda shorts after the US entered World War II. In 1942, 90% of Walt Disney's 550 employees were making war-based films.

1014.   Although Mickey Mouse was the most popular animated character during the 1930s, he was overshadowed in the 1940s by Donald Duck and Goofy. The story of Mickey and the Beanstalk was inserted into this movie to help Mickey Mouse regain his popularity.

1015.   Mickey and the Beanstalk was originally called The Legend of Happy Valley.

1016.   This was the first time where Mickey, Donald, and Goofy starred in a cartoon since The Whalers in 1938.

1017.   This was the last time that Walt Disney voiced Mickey Mouse in an animated feature.

Ghost in the Shell
1995

1018. Bryan Cranston voices Dr. Wills. Cranston is best-known for playing Walter White in Breaking Bad.

1019. The Matrix copied many shots from this film.

1020. The film is based on the 1989 manga series. It originally ran for 18 months.

1021. The creator of the manga, Shirow Masamune, is so shy, it took him a year to agree to be interviewed after the film was a success.

1022. Although the film is dark and gritty, the manga is more comedic and silly.

1023. Motoko rarely blinks. The director did this intentionally so she would appear more doll-like.

1024. The film takes place in 2029.

1025. The tagline is "It found a voice... now it needs a body."

1026. The film was re-released in 2008. This version has computer-generated images in certain shots. This version is called Ghost in the Shell 2.0.

1027. The writer based the philosophy of the story on animism; the belief that all objects have souls.

1028. This was the first anime ever funded by the UK, the US, and Japan. It was also the first anime to be released in the US, the UK, and Japan simultaneously.

1029. The song in the credits was played by the band, U2.

1030. The Japanese title is Mobile-Armoured Riot Police.

1031. The film cost $10 million. It only made $515,905 at the box office.

1032.   Steven Spielberg said this movie has one of the best stories ever. He incorporated the idea of a robot having a soul for his 2001 film, AI.

1033.   Scarlet Johansson plays the main character in the live-action 2017 film, Ghost in the Shell. The role nearly went to Margot Robbie.

1034.   Although Motoko looks like a woman, she acts gender-neutral. According to the writer, Motoko is feminine but not female.

1035.   The sequel, Ghost in the Shell: Innocence, was released in 2004.

1036.   The film spawned an animated series called Ghost in the Shell: Stand Alone Complex in 2002. This show spawned a film called Solid State Society in 2006.

1037.   Although the film is Japanese, it was more successful in the Western world than in Japan. The director believes the film didn't do well in Japan because the Internet plays a huge part in the film, which was an alien concept in Japan at the time.

Gnomeo & Juliet
2011

1038.   Hulk Hogan voices the Terrafirminator lawnmower. (That is a sentence I never thought I would write.)

1039.   In the Terrafirminator commercial, the fine print reads –
i)   Not recommended for residential use
ii)   Not recommended for commercial use either
iii)   Do not use vehicle while sleeping
iv)   Not recommended for children under 3
v)   Or 4
vi)   After use, lawn may appear completely destroyed
vii)   Do not be alarmed – this is perfectly normal
viii)   Side effects may include persistent feelings of awesomeness
ix)   In rare instances, some people may explode when viewing the Terrafirminator
x)   Maker of the Terrafirminator will not be held responsible for infidelity caused by the use of this product.

1040.   Ozzy Osbourne voices Fawn. Michael Caine voices Lord Redbrick. Maggie Smith voices Lady Bluebury. Jason Statham voices Tybalt. Dolly Parton voices Dolly Gnome. Stephen Merchant voices Paris. Patrick Stewart voices Bill Shakespeare.

1041.   James McAvoy voices Gnomeo. Ewan McGregor was considered for the role.

1042.   Emily Blunt voices Juliet. Kate Winslet was considered for the role.

1043.   The story takes place in Stratford-Upon-Avon; the birthplace of William Shakespeare. This is where he wrote Romeo & Juliet.

1044.   The moving company is called As U Like It. This is a reference to the Shakespeare play, As You Like It.

1045.   The glue that the Gnomes use is called The Taming of the Glue. This is a reference to the Shakespeare play, The Taming of the Shrew.

1046.   Two houses numbers can be seen which say "2B" and "Not 2B."

1047.   The tagline is "An adventure like you have never gnome."

1048.   One of the trucks is from a company called Tempest Teapot. This is a reference to the Shakespeare play, The Tempest.

1049.   One of the trucks reads Rosencrantz and Guildenstern moving company. Rosencrantz and Guildenstern were two characters in the play, Hamlet.

The Good Dinosaur
2015

1050.   The short, Sanjay's Super Team, was shown in the cinema before this film.

1051.   When the film was announced, it was called The Untitled Pixar Movie about Dinosaurs.

1052.   This film was released a few months after Inside Out. This is the first time that Pixar released two films in the same year.

1053.   The film was supposed to be released on November 27th 2013. It was released on November 25th 2015.

1054.   This film took six years to make.

1055.   Arlo's movements are based on an elephant.

1056.   The tagline is "Little arms big attitude."

1057.   Arlo is the youngest protagonist in a Pixar film.

1058.   Sam Elliot's voices Butch. At one point, the character says, "In the morning, we ride." Sam Elliott's character in Ghost Rider says the same thing.

1059.   This is one of the few films where T-Rexes are not depicted as villains.

1060.   John Ratzenberger cameos in every single Pixar film. He voices Earl in this film and only has one line.

1061.   When Arlo splashes the water after playing with gophers, an octopus appears for a second. This octopus resembles Hank from Finding Dory.

1062.   The scene where Arlo hallucinates was inspired by the pink elephant scene in Dumbo.

1063.   The film cost $200 million. The Good Dinosaur made $332 million at the box office. Since a film needs to make double the budget to be considered a success, The Good Dinosaur is regarded as Pixar's only flop.

1064.   The Pizza Planet truck from Toy Story cameos in nearly every Pixar film...so how do you hide a truck in a film set millions of years ago. The answer – by being sneaky. The asteroid in the opening scene has the same shape as the Pizza Planet Truck.

1065.   This film had more problems than any other production in Pixar history. Many people were fired or replaced including the director, crew and several actors. John Lithgow, Judy Greer, Bill Hader, and Neil Patrick Harris had recorded most or all their dialogue but they were all recast.

The only main actor that wasn't recast was Frances McDormand, who voices Momma. 80 Pixar workers were fired in 2012, while this film was in production. One year later, another 67 people were fired.

The Great Mouse Detective
1986

1066.   Rattigan's painting smiles any time Rattigan references it.

1067.   Vincent Price voices Rattigan. Rattigan's physicality was based directly on Price when he performed over-the-top gestures while recording his voiceover.

1068.   Basil is named after Basil Rathbone. Rathbone played Sherlock Holmes in 14 films. This film is based on the Sherlock Holmes stories.

1069.   John Cleese and Michael Palin were considered for Basil. Both actors starred in the Monty Python series.

1070.   Most animations take four years to make. It only took a year to make this film.

1071.   The original title was Basil of Baker Street.

1072.   A toy of Dumbo can be seen in the toy shop.

The Grinch
2018

1073. The story is based on Dr. Seuss' book, How the Grinch Stole Christmas! Although the Grinch has green fur and white eyes in the film, he has white fur and red eyes in the book.

1074. The tagline is, "Resting Grinch Face."

1075. The film was delayed for two years. The filmmaking was so difficult, the director left in 2018 and the producer had to take over.

1076. All the animation was created in France.

1077. The baseball bat reads, "Theodor." This is the real name of the author who wrote How the Grinch Stole Christmas!

1078. Benedict Cumberbatch provides the voice of the titular character. Although the director wanted Cumberbatch to use his native British accent, Cumberbatch decided to speak in an American accent to match the rest of the cast.

1079. When Donna is chasing the bus, she shouts to the driver, Sam. This is a reference to the film, Speed, when Sandra Bullock's character does the same thing. I'm sure every kid got that reference.

1080. The screaming goat in this film also appeared in Smallfoot.

Happy Feet
2006

1081.   Robin Williams voices Ramon and Lovelace.

1082.   Robin Williams, Huge Jackman, Nicole Kidman, and Brittany Murphy performed all their own singing.

1083.   All the dancers in the film had to go to Penguin School to learn how to move like a penguin.

1084.   The male penguins have an orange spot on their beaks. The females have a pink spot.

1085.   Elijah Wood voices Mumble. The role nearly went to Owen Wilson.

1086.   Mumble's dancing is based on Fred Astaire.

1087.   The film cost $100 million. It made $384 million at the box office.

1088.   A rip-off of the film was made in 2011 called Tappy Toes. Although the front cover of Tappy Toes implies the film is computer-generated, the creators couldn't afford this technology so the film is in 2D.

1089.   The tagline is, "WARNING: May Cause Toe-Tapping."

1090.   Steve Irwin voices Trev the elephant seal. This was Steve Irwin's final film.

1091.   The film and its sequel were directed by George Miller. Miller is best-known for directing the Mad Max franchise.

Happy Feet 2
2011

1092. Brad Pitt voices Will the Krill. Matt Damon voices Bill the Krill.

1093. Sofia Vergara voices Carmen. She is best-known for playing Gloria in Modern Family. Speaking of Gloria...

1094. The musician, Pink, voices Gloria. Jennifer Lopez was considered for the role.

1095. Common voices Seymour.

1096. Hank Azaria voices The Mighty Sven. He voices over a hundred characters on The Simpsons.

1097. This was the last animated film that Robin Williams starred in before his passing.

1098. The tagline is, "Every step counts."

1099. The film cost $135 million. It tanked at the box office since it only made $150 million. This means that it made less than half of its predecessor.

Hercules
2000

1100.   James Woods voices Hades. He said he played the character like a sleazy car salesman.

1101.   James Woods said that Hades is the best character he has ever played. He loves the character so much that he is more than happy to play him for any television show or video game.

1102.   When Hercules enters Phil's hut, he bangs his head off the Argo mast. In Greek mythology, Jason died when the mast hit his head.

1103.   In this story, Hercules' mother is Hera. In Greek myth, his mother was a mortal woman called Alcmene.

1104.   Pegasus is created out of clouds. In Greek myth, he was created from Medusa's blood.

1105.   According to Zeus, Pegasus is made from Cirrus, Nimbostratus, and Cumulus. These are the names of different cloud formations.

1106.   Every time Hercules chops off the Hydra's head, it grows three more. By the end of the battle, the Hydra has 30 heads.

1107.   It took 18 months to animate the four-minute Hydra battle.

1108.   The tagline is "Zero to hero."

1109.   Philoctetes' design is based on his voice actor, Danny DeVito, and Grumpy from Snow White and the Seven Dwarfs.

1110.   Charlton Heston narrates the film.

1111.   Although many big actors auditioned for Phil, Danny DeVito won the role even though he refused to audition.

1112.   Susan Egan voices Megara. She played Belle in Broadway musical of Beauty and the Beast.

1113.   When Hercules seemingly defeats the Hydra, Hades says, "Relax, it's only half-time." Coincidentally, he says this at the halfway-point of the film.

1114.   When the kids are trapped under the boulder, one of them shouts, "Someone call IXII." These are the Roman numerals for 911.

1115.   The Spice Girls were considered for the Muses.

1116.   It took the animators up to 14 hours to animate one frame of the Hydra.

1117.   In the Latin American version of the film, Ricky Martin voices Hercules.

1118.   There are five Muses in the film. In Greek myth, there were nine. The five Muses in this film are called Calliope, Clio, Thalia, Terpsichore, and Melpomene.

1119.   The four Titans are based on the elements – fire, ice, air, and earth. This isn't an Ancient Greek concept and is more fitting to Norse mythology.

1120.   The Fates share an eye. In Greek myth, it is the Graea that share an eye.

1121.   When Hercules becomes well-known, he starts endorsing products and making appearances for money. Although this seems over-the-top, this was exactly what Ancient Greek athletes used to do.

1122.   David Bowie and Willem Dafoe were considered for Hades. The studio offered Jack Nicholson $500,00 to voice Hades. Nicholson said he would only voice the role for $15 million and 50% of all Hades merchandise. The studio refused.
        John Lithgow was cast as Hades and recorded all his dialogue but he was replaced by James Woods.

1123.   Rip Torn voices Zeus. John Goodman was considered for the role.

1124. In Greek myth, the god of the dead is Pluto. Hades is the Roman god of the dead. In Greek myth, Pluto is not evil. His brothers, Zeus and Poseidon, committed far more evil acts.

1125. In the film, the Titans were banished by Zeus. In Greek myth, Zeus' grandfather, Uranus sealed away the Titans. The leader of the Titans was Zeus' father, Cronus.

1126. When Phil meets Hercules, he said, "Two words: I am retired." In Greek, "I am retired." translates as "Eimai syntaxiochos.," which is two words.

1127. Hades' minions are called Pain and Panic. Their names are translated from Phobos and Deimos. Phobos and Deimos were minions of the Greek god of war, Ares.

1128. When Hades is eating worms, the voice-actor, James Woods, was eating a watermelon.

1129. Contrary to popular believe, Hercules is based on a Roman demi-god. His Greek name is Herakles.

1130. In Greek myth, Herakles killed his wife, Megara, after Zeus' wife, Hera, drove him insane.

Horton Hears a Who!
2008

1131.   This is the second Dr. Seuss adaption that Jim Carrey has been a part of. The first adaptation was How the Grinch Stole Christmas.

1132.   This is the first Dr. Seuss adaptation to be fully animated by CGI.

1133.   Steve Carell voices the Mayor.

1134.   Green eggs can be seen at the Mayor's breakfast table. This is a reference to the Dr. Seuss story, Green Eggs and Ham.

1135.   Dr. Seuss said that this story was an allegory to how Hiroshima and Nagasaki were destroyed in World War II but nobody seemed to care because the cities were on the other side of the planet.

1136.   The Grinch cameos as a snowman.

1137.   The tagline is, "Who-mongous!"

1138.   The film was shipped to cinemas under the fake title, 88 Keys.

1139.   The first painting that the Mayor shows Jo-Jo is of the writer, Theodore Geisel. This is Dr. Seuss' real name.

Hotel Transylvania
2012

1140.   Miley Cyrus was cast as Mavis but she dropped out. She was replaced with Selena Gomez.

1141.   The tagline is "Where monsters go to get away from it all."

1142.   CeeLo Green voices Murray.

1143.   The film was pitched in 2002 and has been in development since 2006.

1144.   Dracula is 532.

1145.   Jonathan is named after Jonathan Harker. He was one of the main characters in the novel, Dracula.

1146.   Mavis' favourite foods are worm cakes and scream cheese.

1147.   The werewolf, Winnie, is voiced by Adam Sandler's daughter, Sadie.

1148.   The town's design is based on the birthplace of Vlad the Impaler, Sighisoara.

1149.   Rebecca Sugar worked on the storyboards. She is the creator of the animated series, Steven Universe.

1150.   The Blob is called Steve. Steve was the name of the main character in the film, The Blob.

1151.   Due to copyright concerns, Frankenstein was not allowed to be green nor could he have electrodes on his neck. The producers tried to get around this by putting electrodes on his temples and lightbulbs on his neck but the studio refused.

Hotel Transylvania 2
2015

1152. Nick Offerman voices Grandpa and Megan Mullally voices Grandma. They are married in real life.

1153. The tagline is "Drac's pack is back."

1154. CeeLo Green couldn't reprise his role as Murray as he was busy being arrested. He was replaced by Keegan-Michael Key.

1155. Mel Brooks voices Vlad.

1156. Jonathan's disguise is based on the elderly version of Dracula in the 1992 film, Bram Stoker's Dracula.

1157. The film takes place seven years after the last one.

1158. This is the tenth film where Adam Sandler and Kevin James have worked together.

1159. At the time of its release, Hotel Transylvania 2 was the most successful film that Adam Sandler ever made.

Hotel Transylvania 3:
Summer Vacation
2018

1160.   The film was supposed to come out in September but it was released in July so it wouldn't clash with the release of Goosebumps 2: Haunted Halloween. Ironically, Goosebumps 2 was delayed to October.

1161.   In some countries, the title translates into Monster Vacation.

1162.   This is the fifth animated film by Sony that Andy Samberg has worked on.

1163.   The tagline was, "He's going to need a vacation after this vacation."

How to Train Your Dragon
2010

1164.   The director said Avatar was a huge influence for the look of the film.

1165.   There is a drawing of the flux capacitor in Hiccup's designs. The flux capacitor is the device that makes time-travel possible in Back to the Future.

1166.   David Tennant cameos as Spitelout.

1167.   When the dragons are bringing their prey to the Red Death, one of them is carrying a hippo. The creators have confirmed that this hippo is Gloria from the Madagascar series.

1168.   Christopher Mintz-Plasse voices Fishlegs. Jonah Hill voices Snotlout. Both actors starred in Superbad.

1169.   The hammer that Stoick uses looks similar to Mjolnir; the hammer that Thor uses in the Marvel comics.

1170.   Hiccup is one of the only Vikings that doesn't have a Scottish accent. This was to make Hiccup feel like an outcast.

1171.   Steven Spielberg helped write the scene at the end when Hiccup wakes up in bed.

1172.   Toothless' face was based on Lilo in Lilo & Stitch.

1173.   Stoic is 7ft 2.

1174.   The tagline is "One adventure will change two worlds."

1175.   The film inspired an animated series called Dragons: Riders of Berk. It takes place between this film and the sequel.

1176.   Gerald Butler voices Stoick. He previously played a dragon-slayer in the film, Reign of Fire.

1177.   When Hiccup holds out his hand, Toothless doesn't touch it for a few seconds. This was a glitch and Toothless was meant

to touch Hiccup's hand much sooner. The animators thought
this shot was so perfect, they didn't change it.

1178.   Hiccup is the only character in the story that is left-
handed; another example that shows he's different from
everyone else. When Hiccup saves everyone, all the Vikings
raise their swords with their left hand.   .

How to Train Your Dragon 2
2014

1179.   Most of the story was meant to be saved for the third film.

1180.   The Bewilderbeast's roar is taken from the titular character in the film, Godzilla.

1181.   Cate Blanchett said that Valka's first scene is the best introduction of a character in movie history.

1182.   The film spawned a prequel series called Dragons: Race to the Edge.

1183.   The characteristics of every dragon is a combination of at least five different animals.

1184.   Hiccup had 50 different redesigns before the director decided how he would look.

1185.   Djimon Hounsou voices Drago. He performed a terrifying scream to make Drago's voice sound gravellier. The director liked this scream so much, he made Hounsou do it as Drago's dragon call.

1186.   Drago's face is based on an eagle.

1187.   Gobber is the first gay character in a DreamWorks film.

1188.   Kit Harington voices Eret. Harington is best-known for playing Jon Snow in Game of Thrones. At one point, Astrid says, "Don't you know anything?" to Eret. This is a reference to characters in Game of Thrones saying, "You know nothing, Jon Snow."

How to Train Your Dragon:
The Hidden World
2019

1189.   The film was delayed for a year.

1190.   Jude Law was rumoured to play a role.

1191.   The villain of the last film, Dragon, was meant to return as the main antagonist of How to Train Your Dragon: The Hidden World. This idea was scrapped in the middle of the film's production.

1192.   This is the first DreamWorks Animation trilogy where each film was released by a different studio; the first film was distributed by Paramount, the second film was distributed by 20th Century Fox, and this film was distributed by Universal.

1193.   The tagline is, "Find your way home."

1194.   TJ Miller provided the voice of Tuffnut in the previous films. He was replaced by Justin Rupple after TJ Miller went kinda crazy.

1195.   Jay Barunchel, America Ferrera, and Christopher Mintz-Plasse are the only actors to star in every film and tv adaptation in the franchise.

1196.   Ragnar the Rock's name is a reference to the Norse version of the apocalypse, Ragnarok.

1197.   The film's fake title was Royal Flush.

1198.   Spoilers for the plot were revealed on the preview pages of Amazon. These were taken down soon after.

Howl's Moving Castle
2004

1199.   When Christian Bale saw Hayao Miyazaki's film, Spirited Away, he told Miyazaki that he would play any part in his next film. Miyazaki cast him as the titular character, Howl, in this film.

1200.   The film is based on the book of the same name. It was written by Diana Wynne Jones in 1986. Jones wrote another book called Castle in the Sky, which was also adapted into a film by Hayao Miyazaki.

1201.   War plays a heavy theme in the film. Weirdly, war isn't referenced in the novel.

1202.   Legendary actress, Lauren Bacall, voices the Witch of the Waste.

1203.   At one point, Markl gorges on food. Miyazaki incorporates gorging in most of his films.

1204.   Billy Crystal voices Calcifer.

1205.   Although it's not clear in the film, Sophie is a witch.

The Hunchback of Notre Dame
1996

1206.   Although Quasimodo speaks to the gargoyles, they revert to normal when anyone walks by. Because no one else sees the gargoyles speaking, some fans have theorized that Quasimodo imagines that they can speak after spending too much time in solitude.

This theory doesn't hold up since the gargoyles set traps in the final battle which couldn't have been set up by Quasimodo.

1207.   Tony Jay voices Frollo. Ian McKellen was considered for the role.

1208.   The heretic looks exactly like Jafar in his Old Man disguise from Aladdin.

1209.   Belle from Beauty and the Beast can be seen in a crowd sequence.

1210.   Frollo's horse is called Snowball.

1211.   The staircase that Quasimodo's mother falls on doesn't exist at the Notre Dame cathedral.

1212.   The film mainly takes place in 1502.

1213.   Quasimodo is 20 years old.

1214.   Kevin Kline voices Phoebus. It was his idea to call his horse Achilles because he thought it would be funny to say, "Achilles, heel."

1215.   Jason Alexander voices the gargoyle, Hugo. Charles Kimbrough voices the gargoyle, Victor. Victor Hugo is the author of the novel, The Hunchback of Notre Dame.

1216.   The third gargoyle is Laverne. Originally, he was called Marle, which was Victor Hugo's middle name.

1217.   Demi Moore voices Esmeralda.

1218.   Quasimodo dies in the novel. The filmmakers strongly considered killing him off in this film.

1219.   Quasimodo's mother dies when she is pushed to the ground and hits her head. This is how Esmeralda's mother dies in the novel.

1220.   Many people assume Hugo the gargoyle is based on Pumbaa since his face looks like a pig. However, this gargoyle is based on a real statue in Notre Dame.

1221.   Tom Hulce voices Quasimodo. He played the titular character in the film, Amadeus.

1222.   David Ogden Stiers voices the Archdeacon. Stiers voices Cogsworth in Beauty and the Beast.

1223.   In the novel, Frollo is the Archdeacon.

1224.   When Quasimodo helps Esmeralda flee from the cathedral, Frollo knocks over a statuette of Esmeralda on his table. This indirectly knocks over a statuette of Frollo. This foreshadows that Frollo's obsession with Esmeralda will be his undoing.

1225.   The song, Hellfire, is considered to be the darkest song in Disney history and was nearly cut from the film.

1226.   There were two other animated films that came out in 1996 that were called The Hunchback of Notre Dame. These films were only made to capitalise on the Disney film of the same name.

1227.   Clopin sings the intro. Originally, it was spoken dialogue.

1228.   This is Michael Eisner's favourite film. He was the CEO of Disney from 1984 to 2005.

1229.   The statues that Quasimodo speaks to are grotesques, not gargoyles. A gargoyle is a statue that spews water from its mouth. It's where the word "gargle" comes from.

Ice Age
2002

1230.   At the test screening, children cried when Diego died so the ending was redone so he survived.

1231.   Jack Black voices Zeke.

1232.   Although Scrat is supposed to be a fictional creature, a prehistoric animal was discovered in 2009 that looks like him. This creature is called a Cronopio.

1233.   The cave drawings are exact duplicates of the first cave drawings ever found.

1234.   The drawings in the credits were done by the animators' children.

1235.   The tagline is "Licensed to chill."

1236.   John Leguizamo voices Sid the sloth. He tried 30 voices for the character but nothing sounded right. While watching a documentary about sloths, he learned the creatures store food in their mouth. He then tried to voice the character by pretending he had food in his mouth. The director thought the voice was perfect.

1237.   Manny is referred to as the Neeny Weeny Mammoth, the Moody Mammoth, Manny the Melancholy, Jumbo, and Fat Hair Boy. His real name is Manfred.

1238.   The film was supposed to be a drama, not a comedy.

Ice Age: The Meltdown
2006

1239.   Throughout the film, Scrat is attacked by piranhas and a baby bird. Both of these scenes were supposed to be in the first film but were cut for time.

1240.   Queen Latifah voices Ellie.

1241.   The horned beavers are based on a real animal called Ceratogaulus.

1242.   Will Arnett voices Lone Gunslinger Vulture. He voiced a vulture again in Horton Hears a Who.

1243.   The tagline is "They never Thaw it coming."

1244.   Crash is based on a prairie dog and a meerkat.

1245.   Jay Leno voices Fast Tony.

1246.   Cholly is a chalicothere, which is a distant relative to the horse.

Ice Age: Dawn of the Dinosaurs
2009

1247.   This is the most successful film in the franchise making nearly $887 million.

1248.   Simon Pegg voices Buck.

1249.   Rudy is based on the Baryonyx dinosaur.

1250.   When Manny sees a dinosaur in the playground scene, he shouts, "Nobody move a muscle!" This line was said by Alan Grant in Jurassic Park when he sees a T-Rex.

1251.   The tagline was, "You won't believe your ice."

1252.   Kristin Wiig voices Pudgy Beaver Mom.

1253.   Despite what viewers may believe, the mother dinosaur is an Allosaurus, not a T-Rex. An Allosaurus has a square shaped head while a T-Rex has a triangular shaped head.

Ice Age: Continental Drift
2012

1254.   Peter Dinklage voices Gutt. Gutt is a relative of an ancient ape called the Gigantopithecus Blacki. This primate stood 10ft tall and weight 1,190lbs. It may have been the largest primate to ever live.

1255.   Gutt was supposed to be a bear.

1256.   Rebel Wilson voices Raz the Procoptodon. Procoptodons are related to kangaroos.

1257.   The tagline is "When the Earth falls apart, history's greatest heroes will keep it together."

1258.   When Manny is stuffing his ears with leaves, he is singing the Candy Man Can from the film Willie Wonka & the Chocolate Factory.

1259.   Originally, the story was going to revolve around Manny, Sid, Diego, Ellie, and Scrat being frozen and unthawed in present day. It would've been called Ice Age: Th4w.

Ice Age: Collision Course
2016

1260.   The film was supposed to conclude with Scrat fighting aliens.

1261.   Jessie J voices Brooke.

1262.   Legendary astronomer, Neil deGrasse Tyson, voices Neil deBuck Weasel.

1263.   Jennifer Lopez voices Shira.

1264.   The tagline was, "Kiss your ice goodbye."

1265.   Scrat's storylines parody films such as Alien, Gravity, Prometheus, and The Martian.

The Incredibles
2004

1266.   The short, Boundin', was shown in the cinema before this film.

1267.   In the beginning of the film, Mr. Incredible says, "Fly home, Buddy. I work alone." to IncrediBoy.

When Syndrome casts his mind back to his moment, it doesn't match up the way the scene was shown before. Originally, Bomb Voyage was in the background when Mr. Incredible said this but in Syndrome's memory, Bomb Voyage is nowhere to be seen. This is to show that Syndrome is remembering the moment incorrectly, proving that his mind has become unhinged and he has become completely obsessed with Mr. Incredible.

1268.   Brad Bird is the director. He came up with the idea for The Incredibles from his own experience of trying to balance a career with his family.

1269.   Mr. Incredible is 6ft 7 and weighs 350lbs.

1270.   When Incrediboy says he is Mr. Incredible's biggest fan, you can see that he has coloured in the inside of his mask with marker. A similar technique is used for the Batman films to make the titular character's eyes look more striking.

1271.   The teaser trailer came out 17 months before the film was released. This was the biggest gap between a trailer and the release of the film in history. None of the footage from the teaser trailer was in the finished film.

1272.   Dash's first name is Dashielle.

1273.   The boy on the tricycle is voiced by the director's son.

1274.   Some critics complained that the dynamic of the Incredibles is too similar to The Simpsons. The similarities are due to the fact that Brad Bird was the story consultant for The Simpsons for years. In his own words, "It was my job to make jokes funny."

1275.   The film was nearly called The Invincibles.

1276.   The film's codename was Tights.

1277.   Animators find clothing difficult to animate. As a result, a tailor had to come into Pixar studios and explain how every type of clothing should look and why.

1278.   Syndrome uses a weapon called Zero Point Energy. Astrophysicist, Stephen Hawking, believes that this concept exists (but he calls it the Casimir Effect.)

1279.   Holly Hunter voices Elastigirl. She learned pilot-lingo for the airplane scene to make it more realistic.

1280.   Brad Bird wanted the film to be cel-shaded. The animation during the end credits shows how the film was supposed to look.

1281.   All the Incredibles powers are identical to the Marvel superheroes, the Fantastic Four – Mr. Fantastic, Invisible Girl, Human Torch, and the Thing. Mr. Incredible is superstrong like the Thing. Elastigirl can stretch like Mr. Fantastic. Violet can turn invisible and create forcefields like Invisible Girl. Dash can move at superspeed like the Human Torch.
        The director said this wasn't intentional since he never read the Fantastic Four comics when he was a kid.

1282.   This is the first Pixar film rated PG instead of U.

1283.   John Ratzenberger voices the Underminer. The Underminer is inspired by the Mole Man; the first supervillain the Fantastic Four ever fought. Brad Bird put this in when one of the crewmembers pointed out the similarities between The Incredibles and the Fantastic Four.

1284.   This Incredibles came out a year before the film adaptation of Fantastic Four. Several changes had to be made to the Fantastic Four's story because there were too many similarities to The Incredibles

1285.   Buddy was only supposed to appear at the beginning of the film.

1286.   The story was meant to have a completely different villain called Xerek.

1287.   Jason Lee voices Syndrome. He was cast after the director saw his performance as Azrael in Dogma.

1288.   The film came out two years early.

1289.   Brad Bird cast Samuel L. Jackson as Frozone because he wanted the character to have the coolest voice possible.

1290.   This is the first Pixar film that didn't receive an Oscar nomination for music.

1291.   Bomb Voyage was originally called Bomb Perignon.

1292.   Lucius' wife is called Honey. She is never seen at any point in the film.

1293.   This is the first Pixar film where the main characters are human.

1294.   There are 35 explosions in the movie.

1295.   When Bob returns to his house after rescuing civilians from a fire, he can be heard humming the theme song.

1296.   Edna Mode is based on a costume designer called Edith Head who worked on hundreds of movies for over half a century.

1297.   Elastigirl can stretch 30 metres and be as thin as 1mm.

1298.   The scene where Dash was sent to the principal's office was removed as it wasn't necessary for the plot. However, it was reinserted as the director worried that the story was focusing too much on Mr. Incredible.

1299.   Holly Hunter starred in this film and Batman V Superman: Dawn of Justice. Both films revolve around the collateral damage caused by superheroes.

1300.   When Mr. Incredible and Elastigirl are infiltrating the lair, the music is based on music from the James Bond series.

1301.   In the original story, all the Incredibles could fly except for Mr. Incredible.

1302.   21 people die in this film.

1303.   When Mr. Incredible and Frozone accidentally break into a building, a fire truck is visible. This truck is Red from the movie, Cars.

1304.   Syndrome was inspired by Batman and Robin. Bird thought that Robin could have turned into a villain if he wasn't adopted by Batman.

1305.   When Mr. Incredible marries Elastigirl, Gazerbeam, Metaman, Thunderhead, and Edna Mode can be seen in the audience.

1306.   The story takes place in the 1960s.

1307.   Mr. Incredible's hands are three times bigger than a normal person's.

1308.   The baby is called Jack-Jack. This is the nickname of the director's son.

1309.   The scene where Frozone gets a drink while at gunpoint was inspired by a scene where Samuel L. Jackson's character in Die Hard with a Vengeance is on the phone while being held at gun point.

1310.   Upon its release, The Incredibles was the only Pixar film to win two Oscars.

1311.   Mirage's phone number spells out "SUPERHERO."

1312.   Mr. Incredible works for Insuracare. In the Singapore version of the film, the company is called Black Hearted Insurance Company.

1313.   The superheroes on Syndrome's database include Stormicide, Tradewind, Blitzerman, Apogee, Vectress, Blazestone, Macroburst, Psycwave, Everseer, Phylange, Downburst, Hyper Shock, and Gamma Jack.

1314.   The animators believed this film couldn't be made any sooner since the technology wasn't good enough to render human beings realistically.

1315.   When Brad Bird first approached Pixar to greenlight the film, he was told that it would take ten years to make and would cost a fortune. In the end, the film only cost $92 million. It made $633 million at the box office.

1316.   The action figure of Elastigirl is called Mrs. Incredible because DC Comics owns the copyrights for the name "Elastigirl."

1317.   The DVD came with a short called Jack-Jack Attack.

1318.   The Incredibles live in Metroville. The city is named after Superman's homes; Smallville and Metropolis.

1319.   All extra characters (the other superheroes, the children, the henchmen) have the same design. It is called the Universal Model.

1320.   Spencer Fox voices Dash. He ran around the studio before he had to record scenes where Dash was exhausted.

1321.   Jack-Jack is the only member of the Incredibles' family that makes physical contact with Syndrome.

1322.   Wallace Shawn voices Bob's boss, Gilbert Huph. Shawn voices Rex in the Toy Story movies.

1323.   Dash can run 200mph.

1324.   Brad Bird believes that most superhero movies start with an action scene before the audience has a chance to know the characters. To focus on the characters, Brad decided to begin the film with the superheroes being interviewed.

1325.   Huph's pencils read "Your Life Is In Our Hands."

1326.   This is the first Pixar film where the Pizza Express truck from Toy Story doesn't cameo.

1327.   Syndrome's computer is based on Cerebro from the X-Men comics.

1328.   The DVD has a terrible cartoon that shows the adventures of Mr. Incredible and Frozone. The cartoon also has an audio commentary with the two characters. Most of the commentary involves Frozone complaining that the cartoon changed his skin tone. He says things like, "I'm white? They made me a white guy?!" Mr. Incredible tries to calm him down by saying, "Well... maybe the prints faded."

1329.   There was a petition to get Barack Obama and Michelle Obama to act out the "Where's My Super Suit?" scene.

The Incredibles 2
2018

1330.   The tagline was, "It's been too long, dahlings." (That's not a typo.)

1331.   The short, Bao, was shown in the cinema before this film.

1332.   Phil LaMarr provides the voice of Krushauer and Helectrix. LaMarr is best-known for providing the voice of the lead character in the animated series, Samurai Jack.

1333.   The film cost $200 million. It only took 46 days for the film to make $1 billion.

1334.   The film is 118 minutes long, making it the longest CGI film ever.

1335.   This film came out 14 years after the previous one. This is the largest gaps between a film and its sequel in the history of Pixar.

1336.   The elderly superhero, Reflux, is based on a frog.

1337.   The raccoon is called Rocky.

1338.   Deavor's father meets the superheroes, Fironic and Gazerbeam. Fironic is the superhero that people mistook Syndrome for in the previous film. Gazerbeam was the body that Mr. Incredible found in the cave in the previous film.

1339.   Edna Mode is enraged when she learns that Elastigirl's costume was made by Galbaki. Galbaki was supposed to appear in the film as Edna's rival.

1340.   Voyd is based on Kristen Stewart.

1341.   There was supposed to be a female superhero with shocking powers called Shelectric.

1342.   Craig T. Nelson provides the voice of Mr. Incredible. Nelson is best-known for playing the lead role in Poltergeist. In both films, Craig's character is forced to stay at a motel after his house was destroyed. Another similarity that both films have is his character's child teleports through a different dimension in his house.

1343.   The Underminer is one of the few Pixar villains to achieve his plan without repercussions.

1344.   Jack-Jack has 17 powers – duplication, demon transformation, optic lasers, intangibility, combustion, mass manipulation, shapeshifting, invincibility, levitation, telekinesis, teleportation, flight, electricity emission, liquefication, lead conversion, and photographic reflexes.

1345.   Bob gets frustrated while trying to teach his son maths because he doesn't understand "new math." This is based on a real concept when a new mathematical system was implemented in American schools during the 1960s. It was dropped after students found it too confusing.

Inside Out
2015

1346.   The short, Lava, was shown in the cinema before this film.

1347.   The writers considered having 27 different Emotions including Trust, Surprise, and Pride.

1348.   Riley's clothes get darker as the film progresses to highlight her depression.

1349.   Richard Kind voices Bing Bong. He also voices Bookworm in Toy Story 3 and Molt in A Bug's Life.

1350.   Richard Kind was crying when he said the line, 'Take her to the moon for me, okay?"

1351.   Joy is the only Emotion with no shadow.

1352.   This is the first Pixar film with no villain.

1353.   The film was nearly called State of Mind, Out of Our Mind, Down in the Dumps, HeadQuarters, and Joy.

1354.   The railways in Riley's headquarters are shaped like DNA strands.

1355.   Phyllis Smith voices Sadness. Emma Stone was considered for the role.

1356.   In the original script, Joy was going to team up with Fear, not Sadness.

1357.   According to the film critic website, Rotten Tomatoes, this is the highest rated animated film with a score of 98%.

1358.   Originally, Disgust was male.

1359.   The Emotions are created in this order – Joy, Sadness, Fear, Disgust, and Anger.

1360.   The film won an Oscar for Best Animated Feature.

1361.   Sadness never interacts with any character except Joy and Bing Bong.

1362.   In an early draft, Riley would enter her own mind and interact with the Emotions. In another draft, Joy could enter the real world.

1363.   The film was directed by Pete Docter. He also directed Monsters, Inc.

1364.   In the original script, Riley suffered amnesia while she was lost in the woods. Her Emotions had to work together to get her memories back.

1365.   The Emotions have a bubbly texture. The animators said this was the most difficult thing to render.

1366.   Frank Oz voices Subconscious Guard Dave. Oz is best-known for voicing Yoda in the Star Wars series.

1367.   The Subconscious Guards argue whose hat belongs to who. This is a reference to the hat-swapping scene in the play, Waiting for Godot.

1368.   Kaitlyn Dias voices Riley. She was never supposed to play the character. Originally, it was her job to read the storyboard narration. The animators got use to her voice and asked her to voice the lead role.

1369.   The noises that Riley makes as a baby are taken directly from Boo in the film, Monsters, Inc.

1370.   Riley's father daydreams about football. In some countries, this daydream was changed to ice hockey.

1371.   Nemo appears on a board game called Find Me when Joy and Sadness are in Imagination Land.

1372.   Despite the film's complexity, it was made by 45 animators. That's half the animators that Pixar had on their other films.

1373. Riley's chief emotion is Joy. Her mother's is Sadness and her father's is Anger.

1374. The film cost $175 million. It made $857 million at the box office.

1375. In France, the film is called Vice-Versa.

1376. The newspaper that Anger reads is called The Mind Reader. The articles he reads always relate to what's happening to Riley.

1377. Some of the memory balls in Riley's minds contain scenes from other Pixar films.

1378. The DVD includes the short, Riley's First Date.

1379. Between 2005-2009, Denise Daniels repeatedly pitched Disney an animated show called The Moodsters. It revolved around characters "representing a single emotion with a corresponding colour." In 2017, she took Pixar to court as she believes Inside Out is a rip-off of her pitched show.

The Iron Giant
1999

1380.　Vin Diesel voices the titular role. It was one of his first movie roles.

1381.　The Giant only says 53 words.

1382.　Peter Cullen was considered for the Iron Giant. He is most famous for voicing Optimus Prime in the Transformers franchise.

1383.　Jennifer Aniston voices Annie.

1384.　The director cast Vin Diesel as the Giant because he reminded him of the character himself; Diesel looks intimidating but he has a soothing and gentle voice.

1385.　Hogarth's surname is Hughes. This is an homage to Ted Hughes, who wrote the original story.

1386.　This is the first 2D film that has a 3D character that plays a major part in the story.

1387.　This is not the only time Vin Diesel played a gentle giant with a minimal vocabulary. He voices Groot in Guardians of the Galaxy. Diesel worked with the same sound technician, Doc Kane, for both characters.

1388.　In the original book, the titular character doesn't originate from space. Instead, he comes from the ocean.

1389.　The tentacles that come out of the Giant's back are modelled after the spaceships in The War of the Worlds.

1390.　The film takes place in 1957. This is the same year the director, Brad Bird, was born.

1391.　The Iron Giant is 50ft tall.

1392.　Brad Bird personally animated the scene where Hogarth acts hyper after having an espresso.

1393.   The Iron Giant was designed by Joe Johnston. Johnston personally designed the X-Wing and the AT-AT walkers in the Star Wars series.

1394.   There was an extra scene where the Iron Giant's dreams appeared on a television set that showed his race destroying a planet. This was removed as it was considered too disturbing.

1395.   The Iron Giant's movements are very mechanical at the start. As the film progresses, his movements become more human-like.

1396.   At one point, Hogarth eats a Twinkie filled with whipped cream. The director used to eat this concoction. He called it the Turbo Twinkie.

1397.   Nothing is known about Hogarth's father except he was a fighter pilot.

1398.   The Iron Giant crashes into a town called Rockwell. This is a reference to Roswell; a settlement in Colorado that revolves around alien conspiracies.

1399.   Brad Bird's pitched the film to the studio by asking, "What if a gun had a soul and chose not to be a gun?"

1400.   The Superman comic that Hogarth shows to the Giant is Action Comics #188 from 1954. In this issue, Superman becomes radioactive and is then perceived as a threat to the planet. This story mirrors how people view the Iron Giant.

1401.   The film was supposed to be a musical.

1402.   Pete Townshend was the film's producer. Townshend is the lead guitarist of the band, The Who.

1403.   The novel that this story is based on is called The Iron Man. The film's title was changed so it wouldn't get mixed up with the superhero, Iron Man.

1404.   The studio wanted John Travolta to voice Dean.

1405.   Christopher   McDonald   voices   Kent.   Arnold Schwarzenegger was strongly considered for the role.

1406.   It took a year to animate the Iron Giant in the first scene even though you can barely see him.

1407.   The film was nearly made in 1991 by Don Bluth. Bluth is known for making The Land Before Time, An American Tail, and All Dogs Go To Heaven.

1408.   The Iron Giant had higher ratings than any film distributed by Warner Brothers in 15 years.

1409.   Although it cost $70 million, it only made $31 million back.

1410.   Brad Bird saw audience members wincing at the scene where Hogarth whacks his face into a branch. He said he was proud of this as he finds it very difficult to display pain in a 2D cartoon.

1411.   Ted Hughes wrote the original story to comfort his children after they lost their mother, Sylvia Plath.

1412.   Although the film is drastically different to the original novel, Ted Hughes was very happy with the story that Brad Bird created. Sadly, he never saw the film as he died one year before the film premiered.

1413.   The original novel's official title is The Iron Man: A Children's Story in Five Nights. It was published in 1968 and is only 59 pages long.

1414.   The novel revolves around The Iron Man protecting the world from a continent-sized alien called The Space-Bat-Angel-Demon.

1415.   The Iron Man novel spawned a sequel in 1993 called The Iron Woman. In this book, the Iron Woman punishes humanity for polluting the world.

1416.   The film nearly concluded with the caption, "THE END...or is it?"

1417.   The tagline is "Some secrets are too huge to hide."

1418.   Although the film is 2D, the Giant is 3D. The director made this decision to make the Giant not fit with the other characters since he is an alien.

1419.   SPOILER – At the beginning of the film, the Soviet satellite, Sputnik, makes a beeping sound. During this time, the United States had a hostile relationship with Russia and were worried they could be attacked or invaded at any moment.

At the end of the film, a beeping sound can be heard. It is revealed that this beeping sound is a homing signal so the Iron Giant can reassemble his body. This is supposed to represent that people fear the unknown. People feared the Iron Giant and Sputnik because humanity didn't understand what their purpose was. However, if people tried to understand the Giant, they would've learned that he wasn't a threat.

If Americans tried to communicate with Russia during the 1950s, there would've been a lot less paranoia. The audience was supposed understand all of this from a beep.

Isle of Dogs
2018

1420.   At the time of its release, this was the longest stop-motion ever at 101 minutes.

1421.   This film was directed by Wes Anderson. This is the eight film where Bill Murray has worked with Anderson.

1422.   Although Angelica Huston isn't in the film, she is credited as Mute Poodle.

1423.   Jeff Goldblum provides the voice of Duke. He recorded all his lines over the phone.

1424.   The dogs' hair is made of alpaca wool.

1425.   The title can also be read as "I love dogs."

1426.   In some scenes, the colours are faded and blurred. This is because dogs are colour-blinded so the scenes from the dog's point of view are coloured to match.

1427.   The five main dogs, Chief, Rex, King, Duke, and Boss, have names that mean "leader."

The Jungle Book
1967

1428.   The film is based on the 1894 collection of stories, The Jungle Book. The story of Mowgli is only one of three tales in the book.

1429.   The original book was written by a British Indian called Joseph Rudyard Kipling. He won a Nobel Prize in Literature in 1907.

1430.   The original story spawned a sequel in 1895 called The Second Jungle Book. It was comprised of eight stories. Five of them revolved around Mowgli.

1431.   The original book was so dark, Walt Disney knew it couldn't work as an animated feature unless the tone was made lighter. Disney gave the writer the book and said "the first thing I want you to do is not read it." Many crewmembers have not read the book to this day.

1432.   This is not the first film adaptation of Kipling's novel. The 1942 film, Jungle Book, is the first adaptation of the famous story.

1433.   The tagline is "A swingin' safari of laughs."

1434.   Walt Disney died before the film was released. The crew only took one day off.

1435.   It was believed that if this film failed, Disney would stop releasing animated films. Luckily, The Jungle Book was a huge success.

1436.   Elvis was considered for a role.

1437.   Many sources state that this was the last film that Walt Disney supervised. This isn't true. The last film he supervised was The Happiest Millionaire.

1438.   The Vultures were supposed to be voiced by The Beatles.

1439.   Some critics believed King Louie was a racially insensitive stereotype of African Americans. The actor who voiced King Louie, Louis Prima, is a white man of Italian heritage. He spoke in his normal voice for the character.

1440.   The film was nearly called A Boy, A Bear and A Black Cat.

1441.   The most difficult thing to animate was Shere Kahn's stripes.

1442.   Kaa's song, Trust in Me, was written for Mary Poppins.

1443.   The Mother Wolf is called Raksha. She has no dialogue.

1444.   All the characters' movements are based on the actors who provided their voices.

1445.   In the Rudyard Kipling novel, Kaa is a helpful and friendly snake. Baloo is grumpy and Bagheera is friendly.
          King Louie doesn't appear in the original book at all.
          Shere Kahn has a withered leg, which has left him with the nickname, Lungri, which means "The Lame One." The novel concludes with Mowgli killing Shere Khan by making a buffalo trample over him while Khan is asleep. Mowgli then skins Kahn and dances around the tiger's hide.

1446.   Many characters are named after Hindi words.
   i)   "Baloo" means "bear."
   ii)   "Hathi" means "elephant."
   iii)   "Bagheera" means "panther."
   iv)   "Shere Kahn" means "Tiger King."

1447.   Clint Howard voices the young elephant. Although Howard has starred in over 200 films, he is best-known as the brother of the Ron Howard. He was only eight years old when this film was released.

1448.   Baloo was supposed to have a small part in the film.

1449.   Marvel created a comic book of The Jungle Book in 2007.

1450.   "Mowgli" is supposed to mean "Little Frog."

1451.   The deer that Shere Kahn tries to attack looks like Bambi's mother.

1452.   Renowned actor, Gregory Peck, demanded that The Jungle Book should be nominated for a Best Picture Oscar. The idea that an animated film could be nominated for such an award was unheard of at the time and didn't happen for nearly 25 years.

1453.   Originally, there was going to be a hunter called Buldeo but his character was eventually scrapped.

1454.   Baloo proved so successful as a sidekick, nearly every Disney film has had a sidekick character since.

1455.   Col. Hathi the elephant becomes enraged when his wife, Winifred, suggests that she should lead the herd. In real life, female elephants do lead the herd.

1456.   Verna Felton voices Winifred. This was the last film she ever worked on. She died one day before Walt Disney.

1457.   This wasn't the first film where Verna Felton voiced an elephant. She voices the Elephant Matriarch in Dumbo.

1458.   Sterling Holloway voices Kaa. Holloway also voices the Cheshire Cat in Alice in Wonderland.

1459.   The sequel, The Jungle Book 2, was released in 2003. Haley Joel Osment voices Mowgli, John Goodman voices Baloo, and Tony Jay voices Shere Kahn.

1460.   A short-sighted rhino called Rocky was cut from the film at the last minute.

1461.   The film was directed by Wolfgang Reitherman. He directed many Disney films including 101 Dalmatians, Robin Hood, The Sword in the Stone, The AristoCats, and The Rescuers.

1462.   This is the most successful film in German history.

1463.   Despite what many people believe, black panthers like Bagheera don't exist. Any animal that was mistaken as a black panther was actually a black leopard. If you look at a black leopard closely, you can see it has spots.

1464.   The vulture song, That's What Friends Are For, was supposed to be a rock song.

1465.   Kaa's name is supposed to be pronounced "Kahr" according to the writer.

1466.   The only song that was in the original script that made it into the final cut was The Bare Necessities. The song won an Oscar.

1467.   George Sanders voices Shere Kahn. He is the first Oscar-winning actor to have a role in an animated Disney film.

1468.   In the novel, Shere Kahn has a sidekick called Tabaqui the Cowardly Jackal.

1469.   In the book, Mowgli is the only one who can resist Kaa's hypnotic stare.

1470.   This is one of the most successful films in the history of the UK.

1471.   Bruce Reitherman performed the voice of Mowgli. He is the son of the director. Nowadays, he makes documentaries about wild life.

1472.   Most people mispronounce Mowgli's name. It's pronounced "MAU-glee." This was confirmed by the writer's daughter, Elsie. She never forgave Disney for this mistake.

Klaus
2019

1473.   Despite how the animation appears, the film is 2D, not 3D.

1474.   The town of Smeerensburg is based on a real town in Norway called Smeerenburg. It was a prominent location for whaling during the 17th century.

1475.   Many studios turned down the film because it was "too risky."

1476.   JK Simmons voices the Drill Sergeant and Klaus AKA Santa. Simmons used to work as a mall Santa.

1477.   The film cost $40 million.

1478.   The tagline is, "Welcome to the jingle."

1479.   The residents and buildings of Smeerensburg were designed with sharp angles and triangles to come across as unfriendly. This is a common technique in animation and was used for the dogs in Up and for the character of Jafar in Aladdin.

1480.   Jesper was meant to be a chimney sweep.

1481.   Jesper's name means "treasure."

Kubo and the Two Strings
2016

1482.   The film was inspired by the work of Akira Kurosawa. Kurosawa is often considered to be the greatest film director of all time.

1483.   The first and last thing Kubo's mother says is, "Kubo."

1484.   Kubo's instrument is called a shamisen.

1485.   George Takei voices Hosato. When the chicken has its head sliced off, Hosato says, "Oh my." This is George Takei's catchphrase.

1486.   Kameyo asks Kubo to incorporate a chicken monster into his story. This creature is a part of Japanese mythology and is known as a Basan.

1487.   The end credits song is Regina Spektor's version of the Beatles song, While My Guitar Gently Weeps.

1488.   Some of the crew had to attend origami classes to make the paper scenes look as accurate as possible.

1489.   The Moon Beast is 73ft long.

1490.   The Moon Beast is the first character in a stop-motion film that was entirely created from a 3D printer.

1491.   The tagline is "Be bold. Be brave. Be epic."

1492.   Kubo is inspired by the Ancient Greek poet, Orpheus. Orpehus' music was supposed to be so beautiful, it charmed the animals and caused rocks to move.

1493.   The giant skeleton is the biggest stop-motion puppet in movie history, standing 16ft.

1494.   Art Parkin plays Kubo. He is from Donegal in Ireland. Since he was in his home country at the time of the audition, he read for the role through his mother's iPad and then sent it to the casting director.

1495.   Matthew McConaughey voices Beetle. His character speaks in a neutral voice. McConaughey found this extremely difficult due to his thick Texan accent.

1496.   McConaughey did push-ups before recording any intense scenes.

1497.   Although the film was highly praised, it didn't do well at the box office as it only made $70 million. Since it cost $60 million, it only made a measly $10 million profit.

1498.   The word, "story," is uttered 31 times. It is said 13 times in the last 15 minutes.

1499.   When Art Parkinson was cast as Kubo, the director was disappointed to learn his voice had gotten deeper since he went through puberty. Since Art just finished working with Dwayne "The Rock" Johnson in the film, San Andreas, the director joked that hanging around Johnson made Art hit puberty at super-speed.

Kung Fu Panda
2008

1500. Jackie Chan voices Monkey. He recorded his lines in English, Mandarin, and Cantonese in five hours.

1501. Each of the Furious Five's fighting style is based on their species – tiger, mantis, crane, monkey, and viper.

1502. Originally, Mantis was supposed to be revealed to be a secondary villain.

1503. Po is in awe when he sees the relics in the Jade Palace. His reaction is based on one of the directors when he visited Skywalker Ranch as a kid and saw all the props from the Star Wars films.

1504. James Hong voices Ping. Ping owns a noodle shop. Hong's father owned a noodle shop in real life.

1505. The tagline is "Prepare for awesomeness."

1506. Ping was meant to be Po's boss, not his step-father.

1507. The prison is called Chor Ghom Prison. This is Cantonese for "sit in prison."

1508. In the original script, Shifu believed he was the Dragon Warrior.

1509. It took six months to animate Oogway's final scene.

1510. Oogway was supposed to be a cocky mobster-like character.

1511. The scene where Tai Lung fights Po on the rooftops was inspired by fight scenes in Crouching Tiger, Hidden Dragon.

1512. "Oogway" is Chinese for "Tortoise." "Shifu" is Chinese for "teacher-master." "Tai Lung" means "Great Dragon."

1513. Po's fighting style is Bear.

1514. Tai Lung is a snow leopard. Snow leopards prey on pandas, making him the perfect antagonist for Po.

1515. Tai Lung needed to be revised since he was considered too sympathetic to be a villain.

1516. The animators said that Kung Fu Hustle was a massive influence on this film.

1517. Po's mother was originally going to play a major part in the film.

1518. The animators took a six-hour kung fu class to get an idea of how the martial arts should be portrayed. They also spent years studying Chinese art and watching tons of kung fu movies.

1519. Chinese film distributors said the film depicts ancient China more accurately than most Chinese films.

1520. The markings on Viper's back are Chinese poetry.

1521. Every time an animator finished a scene, they were rewarded with a fortune cookie.

1522. Kai appears in Po's dream in the beginning. Kai is the main villain in Kung Fu Panda 3.

1523. Angelina Jolie voices Tigress. Jolie has a tiger tattoo on her back.

1524. Tigress' markings are designed to resemble make-up.

1525. Chop Kick Panda is a 2011 rip-off of Kung Fu Panda. The whole film was made with Flash animation.

Kung Fu Panda 2
2011

1526.   Jean Claude Van Damme voices Croc. Croc does the splits in one scene. This is a signature move for Van Damme.

1527.   This is the first animated film that Jean Claude Van Damme has performed in.

1528.   Gary Oldman voices the main villain, Shen.

1529.   Shen's fighting style is called Cai Li Fo. This technique involves fighting with a metal fan. Instead of a fan, Shen uses his feathers.

1530.   Shen was supposed to appear in the first film as an evil mayor.

1531.   The tagline is "Ska2oosh."

1532.   This film was directed by Jennifer Yuh Nelson. At the time of its release, it was the most successful film ever directed by a woman.

1533.   Charlie Kaufman wrote some scenes. Kaufman has written Eternal Sunshine of the Spotless Mind, Being John Malkovich, and Adaptation.

1534.   James Hong describes his character, Ping, as "A Jewish mom and Chinese dad combined."

1535.   The original title was going to be Pandemonium. Another potential title was The Kaboom of Doom.

Kung Fu Panda 3
2016

1536.   Originally, Mads Mikkelson voiced the main villain, Kai. He was replaced with JK Simmons.

1537.   The main villain in each film is supposed to represent a different challenge for Po –
i)   Tai Lung is a physical opponent
ii)   Shen is a mental opponent
iii)   Kai is a spiritual opponent.

1538.   The animators went to a panda reserve in China to get a sense of how the creatures moved. They noticed that the pandas rolled to their destination and so, incorporated it into the film.

1539.   Kai's minions are called Jombies. Their animation skips frames so they appear more erratic.

1540.   Kai was supposed to have four arms.

1541.   The tagline is "The weight is over."

1542.   Originally, Rebel Wilson voiced Meimei.

1543.   One of the pandas is based on Hodor from the TV series, Game of Thrones.

Lady and the Tramp
1955

1544.   The film cost $4 million. It made $93 million. At the time, this was the most successful Disney cartoon since Snow White and the Seven Dwarfs.

1545.   Human faces are rarely seen. This was done intentionally to maintain the dogs' perspective.

1546.   Barbara Luddy voices Lady. Luddy voices Merryweather in Sleeping Beauty.

1547.   The setting was partly inspired by Disney's hometown, Marceline in Missouri.

1548.   A dream sequence showing dogs walking humans was scrapped after it received negative feedback.

1549.   One newspaper headline reads, "Disaster Seen As Catastrophe Looms." This headline has appeared in many newspapers in animated films including The Iron Giant and The Incredibles.

1550.   The trailer spoiled the ending.

1551.   This is the first animated film that Disney made from scratch since Dumbo.

1552.   Peggy Lee voices Darling. This is the first time a famous person played a pivotal role in an animated film.

1553.   This is one of the few Disney films with no villain.

1554.   Walt Disney hated the spaghetti-eating scene. It is now one of the most iconic moments in film history.

The Land Before Time
1988

1555.   This film has at least 13 sequels. This is the only film in the series that isn't a musical.

1556.   Five dinosaurs in this film were already extinct at the time this story takes place.

1557.   George Lucas and Steven Spielberg produced the film. It is the only time that Lucas and Spielberg produced a film outside of the Indiana Jones franchise.

1558.   George Lucas and Steven Spielberg wanted the film to have no dialogue.

1559.   Ten minutes of the film was lost.

1560.   19 scenes were cut or heavily trimmed as they were considered too scary.

1561.   Littlefoot is an Apatosaurus, Spike is a Stegosaurus, Petrie is a Pteranodon and Ducky is a Parasaurolophus. Cera is supposed to be a Triceratops but she is actually a Torosaurus.

1562.   Cera was supposed to be male called Bambo.

1563.   Spielberg said the film is like "Bambi with dinosaurs."

1564.   Littlefoot was originally going to be called Thunderfoot.

1565.   This film contains 29 dinosaurs.

1566.   The dinosaurs use different terminology for certain words –

    i)   The Mountain That Burns - Volcano
    ii)   The Bright Circle – The Sun
    iii) The Great Earth Shake - Earthquake
    iv) Sharp-tooth - Tyrannosaur
    v)   Long Neck - Apatosaurus
    vi) Hopper – Frog

Legend of the Guardians: The Owls of Ga'Hoole
2010

1567.   This is the first non-R rated film directed by Zack Snyder. Snyder is best known for directing 300, Batman V Superman, and Dawn of the Dead.

1568.   Jim Sturgess plays Soren. This is the first 3D animated film he ever saw.

1569.   Hugh Jackman was originally supposed to star.

1570.   Helen Mirren voices Nyra.

1571.   The film is based on Kathryn Lasky's book series, Guardians of Ga'Hoole. The series began in 2003 and is composed of 24 books.

The Lego Batman Movie
2017

1572.   Billy Dee Williams voices Harvey Dent. He plays the same character in Tim Burton's film, Batman.

1573.   Batman suggests calling his team the Fox Force 5. This is the title for Mia Wallace's failed TV pilot in the film, Pulp Fiction.

1574.   In the beginning, Batman says, "You want to get nuts? Let's get nuts!" Bruce Wayne says this line to the Joker in the 1989 film, Batman.

1575.   Mexican director, Guillermo del Toro, nearly voiced Bane.

1576.   Will Arnett uses a gravelly voice for his portrayal as Batman. He uses the same voice to his children when they are naughty.

1577.   Zach Galifianakis voices the Joker. The role nearly went to Steve Buscemi.

1578.   Eddie Izzard voices Voldermort.

1579.   Ralph Fiennes voices Alfred. He nearly played Batman in Batman Forever.

1580.   The Batmobile's horn plays the theme song from the 1966 TV series, Batman.

1581.   King Kong, Medusa, the Wicked Witch of the West, Gremlins, and the Kraken can be seen in The Phantom Zone.

The Lego Movie
2014

1582.   The word "Lego" is never said at any point.

1583.   The wizard is called Vitruvius. He is named after an architect from Ancient Rome. His name means "Master Builder." He was the inventor of the elevator.

1584.   Vitruvius' staff is a chewed-up lollipop.

1585.   Will Arnett is the first Canadian to portray Batman.

1586.   When something goes wrong, Batman usually says, "Oh, come on!" Will Arnett's character in Arrested Development usually says the same thing.

1587.   There are 183 unique characters in the film.

1588.   The original title was Lego: The Piece of Resistance.

1589.   The last third of the film was supposed to be entirely live-action.

1590.   To make the Lego look realistic, the blocks are covered in scratches, fades, and fingerprints.

1591.   Chris Pratt voices Emmet. The role nearly went to Robert Downey Jr.

1592.   The name, "Emmet," is derived from the word, "ant." Ants are known for efficiently working as a team to build huge constructs.

1593.   Batman throws 15 Batarangs at the red button in the "First try" scene.

1594.   Lord Business is designed to look like a tie.

1595.   The animators never "cheated" with the Lego blocks. Everything designed in the film would look the same if it was made of Lego.

1596.   The story revolves a group of people from different dimensions who band together to defeat a villain who lives in a colossal tower and wishes to control the world with a magical artefact. This concept is the same as Stephen King's series, The Dark Tower.

1597.   The film inspired a Simpsons episode that is mostly made of Lego.

1598.   Liam Neeson voices Good Cop, Bad Cop, and Pa.

1599.   This is the first film to depict both Batman and Superman.

1600.   When Lord Business captures Wonder Woman, he places her in handcuffs. Some viewers thought this didn't make sense since Wonder Woman can easily break out of handcuffs. But in the original comics, Wonder Woman became powerless when she was bound by a man.

1601.   Batman looks angry when he sees the clown in Cloud Cuckoo Land. This is because the clown reminds Batman of the Joker.

1602.   In Aristophanes' 414BC play, The Birds, Mr. Trusting and Mr. Hopeful build a perfect city in the sky called Cloud Cuckoo Land. In this film, Cloud Cuckoo Land is a place with no rules or limitations.

1603.   Vitruvius gives Wyldstyle many nicknames including Geminizzle, Neversmile, Freakface, Darkstorm, and Snazzypants.

1604.   One of the lands in the movie is called Middle Zealand. It is a reference to Middle-Earth in The Lord of the Rings. That movie was shot in New Zealand.

1605.   Emmett has a poster for a film called Macho and the Nerd. This is the Russian name for the movie, 21 Jump Street.

1606.   This is the fourth film that Morgan Freeman has starred in where Batman played a key role.

1607.   The introduction takes place 8½ years in the past. This references the scene where Finn discovers the basement when he's 8½.

1608.   Morgan Freeman said that Will Arnett's depiction of Batman is the best performance of the character.

1609.   Denzel Washington was considered for Vitruvius.

1610.   The giant bricks at the end are made of Duplo. Duplo is a Lego set designed for toddlers.

1611.   The story is very similar to The Matrix and The Matrix Reloaded.

1612.   When Wyldstyle talks about the different Lego worlds, she quickly refers to "a bunch of others we don't need to mention." This bunch includes Bionicle and Speed Racer. Neither of these sets sold well in the Lego line. Speed Racer does appear later in the film.

1613.   Chris Pratt distracts the villains by dancing and beat-boxing. His character does the same thing in the film, Guardians of the Galaxy.

1614.   Elizabeth Banks voices Wyldstyle. Weirdly, she played a character called Wild Style in the TV series, Modern Family.

1615.   Emma Stone was considered for Wildstyle.

1616.   After the first Everything Is Awesome scene, a title card reads "5 Hours Later." This title was written with real Lego and is one of the few non-CGI shots in the film.

1617.   MetalBeard's Six Laws of the Sea are -
i)   Never place your rear end on a pirate's face.
ii)   Never release a Kraken.
iii)   Never put ye hand in a clam's mouth.
iv)   Always abandon a lost cause.
v)   Jolly Rogers are not for eating.
vi)   Never wear a dress on Tuesday.

1618. Vitruvius wears a tie-dye shirt and blue jeans under his robe.

1619. If the film was done with stop-animation, it would've taken ten years to make and required 15 million Lego bricks.

1620. It was extremely difficult to secure the rights to use Superman in this film.

1621. Batman's license plate is BAT2DBONE.

1622. Originally, Metalbeard was going to be Emmet's partner, not Batman.

1623. The film cost $60 million. At the time of its release, The Lego Movie was the most successful animated film released by Warner Bros, making $460 million.

1624. Cobie Smulders voices Wonder Woman. She was in the running to play the same character in the film, Wonder Woman.

1625. Channing Tatum voices Superman. Jonah Hill voices Green Lantern. Nick Offerman voices Metalbeard. All these actors starred in 21 Jump Street.

1626. Charlie Day voices Benny the 1980-Something Space Guy. His helmet is cracked and worn-out. This is a reference to the fact that this Lego figure was criticized because it's helmet easily cracked.

1627. Liam Neeson wasn't available at the same time as Will Ferrell so they recorded their scene on the phone.

1628. The scriptwriters intended there to be a song called Everything is Awesome before the lyrics were written. They wanted the song to be the most annoyingly catchy song possible.

1629. When Emmet flies through the air after the Wild West scene, you can see a pig in the background. When the pig hits the ground, it explodes into sausages.

1630.   Lord Business was to be called Black Falcon.

1631.   In an early script, R2-D2 and Indiana Jones were main characters.

1632.   Lego sales boosted by 15% shortly after the film was released.

1633.   Will Forte voices Abraham Lincoln. He is incorrectly called "Orville Forte" in the credits.

1634.   This is the first film to feature Wonder Woman.

1635.   The credits were done with stop-motion. It took over a year to complete the animation.

1636.   C-3PO and Lando Carissian are voiced by the actors who portrayed them in the Star Wars films.

1637.   When Wyldstyle flips a table in the Melting Room, a schedule can be seen on the bottom that reads, "DON'T FORGET TO CLEAN THE LASER!!" This is followed by another note that reads, "HOW ABOUT YOU CLEAN IT."

1638.   There was going to be a scene where every character that Johnny Depp has ever played would meet up and talk to each other.

The Lego Movie 2:
The Second Part
2019

1639.   Margot Robbie provides the voice of Harley Quinn. She played the same character in Suicide Squad.

1640.   Stephanie Beatriz provides the voice of Sweet Mayhem. Beatriz has a cut on her right eyebrow. She received this cut as a child from a piece… of Lego. How ironic.

1641.   The tagline is, "They come in pieces."

1642.   The film was delayed for two years.

1643.   The film was directed by Mike Mitchell. He provides the voice of the Octopus.

1644.   During the Gotham City Guys song, every actor who has played Batman in a movie is referenced.

1645.   Rex Dangervest is a "galaxy defending archaeologist, cowboy, and raptor trainer. This is a reference to the characters Chris Pratty played in The Magnificent Seven, Guardians of the Galaxy, and Jurassic World.

1646.   The first film received criticism since Emmet was considered the hero despite the fact that Wildstyle did most of the work. This is addressed in this film.

1647.   Richard Ayoade plays Ice Cream Cone. Noel Fielding plays Balthazar. Both actors worked together in The IT Crowd and The Mighty Boosh.

1648.   Sweet Mayhem is based on the Lego friends "mini-dolls."

Lilo & Stitch
2002

1649.   "Lilo" means "generous one." It can also mean "lost," which suits Lilo, since he is on an alien planet.

1650.   Tia Carrere voices Nani. She helped the writers with the Hawaiian dialogue and accents. Carrere is best-known for playing Cassandra in Wayne's World.

1651.   Jason Scott Lee voices Kawena. He also helped the writers with the accents. Lee is best-known for playing Mowgli in the 1994 live-action film, The Jungle Book.

1652.   Two of the aliens are based on the Winnie the Pooh characters, Piglet and Tigger.

1653.   Ving Rhames voices Cobra. His character is based on Marcellus Wallace from Pulp Fiction, which Rhames played.

1654.   The sequel, Stitch! The Movie, was released in 2003. The show, Lilo & Stitch: The Series was released in 2003.

1655.   The sequel, Lilo & Stitch 2: Stitch Has A Glitch, was released in 2005. Despite the fact it's called Lilo & Stitch 2, it is the third Lilo & Stitch film.

1656.   Leroy & Stitch was ANOTHER sequel which was released in 2006. It was supposed to conclude the story of the animated series.

1657.   Only two animated Disney films made a profit in the 2000s; this film and The Princess and the Frog.

1658.   Lilo is six years old. Her voice actress, Daveigh Chase, was nine when she started voicing the role.

1659.   Stitch doesn't have pupils. This made it very difficult to show what emotion Stitch is feeling since he can barely talk. This forced the animators to be more creative with Stitch's gestures.

The Lion King
1994

1660. This film was made by the Disney Team B. This was supposed to be the "filler" Disney film while the "superior" Team A was making Pocahontas. Disney thought Pocahontas was going to be a success and The Lion King was going to fail. The Lion King is considered to be the greatest Disney film ever.

1661. Can You Feel the Love Tonight? was meant to be sung by Timon and Pumbaa.

1662. In the original backstory, Mufasa accidentally cut his brother's face while they were young. This left him with the nickname, Scar.

1663. The director, Rob Minkoff, stood in for Mufasa before James Earl Jones recorded his lines. The crew said Minkoff does an incredible impression of Jones.

1664. Although it is common knowledge that the film is heavily inspired by William Shakespeare's play, Hamlet, it is also based on the Ancient Egyptian story of Osiris. Osiris was killed by his evil brother, Seth. Osiris' son, Horus, exiles himself until his father's ghost beckons him to return and exact revenge on Seth.

   The story is similar to a Niger Congo tale about a king called Sundiata, (which means "lion king,") who was banished from his home after his father died. He eventually returns and battles the evil wizard king who has taken over his former home.

   Another story the film resembles is Kimba the White Lion. The stories are so similar that Matthew Broderick thought The Lion King was a remake when he was cast as Simba.

1665. The first scene was supposed to include narration that explained who each of the main characters are.

1666. The translation of The Circle of Life is, "Here comes a lion, Father/ Oh, yes, it's a lion / Here comes a lion, / Oh yes, it's a lion / A lion We're going to conquer / A lion A lion and a leopard come to this open place."

1667. Zazu's name is misspelt as Zasu in the credits.

1668.   Rafiki's song translates into, "Thank you very much, squash banana, you're a baboon and I'm not."

1669.   In the original draft, Scar was simply an evil lion and wasn't related to Mufasa.

1670.   To animate the hyenas marching, the crew watched footage of Nazis goose-stepping.

1671.   In the film, lions are graceful, powerful animals and hyenas are mindless scavengers. Ironically, it is almost the opposite in real life. Hyenas are ferocious and very intelligent. Lions, on the other hand, scavenge the animals that hyenas kill.

1672.   There are anteaters in the I Can't Wait To Be King scene, even though these animals don't live in Africa.

1673.   A song called The Morning Report was completed but left out. It was reinserted into the film when it was released on DVD. It is sung by Zazu and Simba.

1674.   Mufasa wasn't supposed to return as a ghost. It was thought up at the last minute and was the final thing drawn for the movie.

1675.   Jeffrey Katzenberg was the chairman of Walt Disney Studios from 1984-1994. This was the last film supervised by Jeffrey Katzenberg before he created Disney's competitor, DreamWorks.

1676.   Scar's face is based on Jeremy Irons' face.

1677.   The creators of the film loved The Circle of Life intro so much, they used it as the trailer for the movie. This was the first time that Disney used a complete scene for a movie trailer.

1678.   Disney animators ventured to Africa to study how the animals interacted with each other.

1679.   Most of the characters' names are Swahili words.
i)   Simba means "lion."

ii)   "Sarabi" means "mirage."
iii)   "Rafiki" means "friend."
iv)   "Pumbaa" means "simpleton."
v)   "Shenzi" means "barbarian."
vi)   "Banzai" means "skulk."

1680.   When Timon is eating bugs, one of the insects in the background has Mickey Mouse ears.

1681.   Scar's claws are never retracted at any point.

1682.   The stampede scene took three years to animate.

1683.   When the stampede begins, the camera zooms in on Simba's face. This one shot took a year to animate.

1684.   In the original script, Timon and Pumbaa were friends with Simba from the very beginning.

1685.   This film has the highest rating on IMDB of any animated Disney film that wasn't made by Pixar.

1686.   In an early draft, Scar was going to kill Simba. Scar would say, "Good night, sweet prince." before throwing Simba into the fiery pit. This quote is from Hamlet, which was one of the main inspirations for this film.

1687.   Pumbaa regularly rubs his belly. The animator decided to incorporate this into the film after watching his pregnant wife do the same thing.

1688.   When Mufasa tells Simba about the Great Kings of the Past, one of the star alignments is of Mickey Mouse.

1689.   Despite the film's legacy, it was very cheap. It only cost $45 million. The Lion King made over $900 million at the box office. At the time, it was the most successful animated film ever, the most successful hand-drawn animated film ever, and the most successful film of the year apart from Jurassic Park.

1690.   When Mufasa and Simba talk about the stars, the constellation for Leo is clearly visible. Leo represents the lion.

1691.   This was the first Disney cartoon to be dubbed into Zulu.

1692.   Although Rafiki is supposed to be a mandrill, he has a tail, which mandrills lack.

1693.   Simba's mother, Sarabi, was supposed to sing a song called The Lion in the Moon but it was cut.

1694.   Hakuna Matata wasn't in the original script.

1695.   The stampede was so difficult to animate, the creators had to write a new program to control the wildebeests' movements.

1696.   The film won two Oscars. Elton John won an Oscar for Best Original Song and Hans Zimmer won for Best Original Score.

1697.   Simba's mane was inspired by Jon Bon Jovi's hair.

1698.   There were 15 different versions of Can You Feel the Love Tonight?

1699.   The film inspired the Broadway musical which opened in 1997. It won six Tony Awards, including Best Musical.

1700.   None of the lion roars were from actual lions. Frank Welker provided all the lion roars himself by screaming into a trash can.

1701.   In 1994, Disney made over a billion dollars from Lion King merchandise.

1702.   An earthquake occurred near Walt Disney Studios in 1994 which forced the animators to complete their drawings at home.

1703.   According to the director, this film takes place before humanity existed.

1704.   The film inspired a sequel in 1998 called The Lion King 2: Simba's Pride. Since The Lion King is based on Hamlet, the creators of the sequel decided to maintain the Shakespeare motif and based the sequel's story on Romeo and Juliet.

1705. The film inspired a sequel/prequel/sidequel called The Lion King 1½ which revolves around Timon and Pumbaa before, during, and after the events in The Lion King. It is based on the play, Rosencrantz and Guildenstern Are Dead.

1706. The film inspired an animated series called Timon & Pumbaa which ran for five seasons.

1707. The gopher was supposed to be a naked mole rat but the artists couldn't draw it properly.

1708. During the song, Be Prepared, Jeremy Irons roars, "You won't get a sniff without me!" He strained his throat so much when he said that line that he lost his voice and couldn't continue the song.

The rest of the song is voiced by Jim Cummings who sings in Jeremy Irons voice perfectly. The transition is so seamless, it's impossible to notice.

The Lion King
(Remake)
2019

1709.   Despite being called "the live-action version of The Lion King," everything in the film is animated except for the very first shot.

1710.   Seth Rogen provides the voice of Pumbaa. Rogen said his singing was so terrible, his coach was banging his head off the wall in frustration during their sessions. Despite this, Rogen's performance is often seen as the highlight of the film.

1711.   Chiwetel Ejiofor plays Scar. Jeremy Irons, who provided the voice of Scar in the original film, said he was interested in reprising the role.

1712.   Zazu's dialogue referring to Mufasa's past was taken from the Broadway version of The Lion King.

1713.   Benedict Cumberbatch turned down the role of Scar.

1714.   Billy Eichner won the role of Timon without auditioning. He used to be a bartender at the Broadway version of The Lion King.

1715.   Be Prepared was nearly cut since the song is often associated with Nazism.

1716.   Unlike the original film, Timon walks on all fours like a real meerkat.

1717.   There are 86 species in the film.

1718.   The hyenas are called Azizi and Kamari. "Azizi" means "moonlight" and "Kamari" means "mighty."

1719.   Beyonce plays Nala. She said The Lion King was the first film that made her cry.

1720.   The film is set in Tanzania.

1721.   The director, Jon Favreau did the motion-capture for the actors if they were unavailable.

1722.   Many people have complained how it's non-sensical for the song, "Can You Feel the Love Tonight?" to be sung... in the daytime.

1723.   The film was animated by 130 animators over 30 countries.

1724.   Tony Bancroft animated Pumbaa in the original film. He said the remake was "the 'meh' heard around the world."

1725.   The animators didn't add human expressions to the animals as it would look "weird." Instead, the animators tried to make the characters convey emotion through their body language.

1726.   The film cost $260 million. It made $1.6 billion at the box office. The original film made $968 million at the box office. This film made more money in the first week.

The Little Mermaid
1989

1727.   Prince Eric was played by Christopher Barnes. He was only 16 when he recorded his lines. He also voiced Peter Parker in the 1994 cartoon, Spider-Man.

1728.   The story is based on the Danish fairy-tale of the same name. Weirdly, the film was panned by critics in Denmark because it was too different from the original story. The Queen of Denmark, Margrethe, defended the film by saying the writer "didn't know how to end his stories, anyway."

1729.   In the opening scene, Mickey Mouse, Goofy, Donald Duck, and Kermit the Frog can be seen in the crowd.

1730.   In Greek mythology, Poseidon was the king of the sea. In this film, the king of the sea is Poseidon's son, Triton.

1731.   Ursula is a Cecaelia; half-human, half-octopus.

1732.   An actor had to dress up as Ursula so the animators could draw her movements correctly. The actor was a man.

1733.   Sherri Stoner modelled for Ariel. She was also the model for Belle in Beauty and the Beast.

1734.   Sherri Stoner has lots of habited that were incorporated into Ariel such as blowing her hair, biting her lip, and playing with her hair.

1735.   Although Part of Your World is an iconic song, Ariel never says those words at any point. Instead, she says "Part of That World."

1736.   Part of Your World was nearly cut.

1737.   The film had more special effects than any Disney film since Fantasia.

1738.   Ariel's sisters are called Attina, Alana, Aquata, Arista, Adella, and Andrina.

1739.   The colour of Ariel's tail is called....ariel.

1740.   Originally, Disney wasn't interested in the film as they thought it was too similar to the mermaid comedy, Splash, which only came out in 1984.

1741.   Jodi Benson voices the red-headed mermaid, Ariel. Weirdly, Benson has voiced three redheaded characters who fall in love with males not of her own species – Thumbelina, Balto, and The Little Mermaid.

1742.   The tails of the seven daughters of Triton correspond with the colours of the rainbow – red, orange, yellow, green, blue, indigo, and violet.

1743.   Patrick Stewart was supposed to voice Triton.

1744.   Jim Carrey auditioned for Eric.

1745.   The Grand Duke and the King from Cinderella appear at Ariel's wedding.

1746.   Ariel is 16.

1747.   The director wanted Bea Arthur to voice Ursula but she turned it down. Roseanne Barr also auditioned for the role.

1748.   Ursula only has six tentacles.

1749.   There is an iconic shot of Ariel jumping onto a rock as the water splashes behind her. This shot was inspired by the statue of The Little Mermaid which can be found in Copenhagen.

1750.   Ariel's father is the son of Poseidon. Poseidon's brother, Zeus, had a son called Hercules. This means that Ariel and Hercules are related.

1751.   Michael Richards was considered for Scuttle the seagull. Richards is best-known for playing Kramer in Seinfeld.

1752.   Ursula's eels are called Flotsam and Jetsam.

1753.   In the final battle, Ursula turns into a giant. This was a last-minute idea.

1754.   Ariel's wedding dress is based on Princess Diana's wedding gown.

1755.   Pat Carroll voices Ursula. She based the character's personality on a sleazy car salesman.

1756.   Ariel is the first Disney Princess to have red hair. She is also the first Disney Princess to have siblings.

1757.   Originally, Ursula was going to look more like a dragonfish.

1758.   Walt Disney bought the rights for the film in 1941. Walt intended to make the story very dark just like the original story. Sadly, he had The Little Mermaid shelved only two years later.

1759.   The shark is called Glut.

1760.   Ariel and Sebastian are named after two characters from William Shakespeare's The Tempest.

1761.   This was the first Disney film to win an Oscar since Bedknobs and Broomsticks in 1971.

1762.   There is a rumour that Prince Eric is related to Prince Philip from Sleeping Beauty.

1763.   In one draft, Ursula was Triton's sister.

1764.   Despite what many people believe, Sebastian doesn't speak with a Jamaican accent. Sebastian has a Trinidadian (or Trini) accent.

1765.   Originally, Sebastian was going to be British.

1766.   Ursula is based on the drag performer, Divine.

1767.   Flounder's fish species doesn't exist.

1768.   Ursula's gestures are based on the villain from The Rescuers, Madame Medusa.

1769.   The film spawned a sequel in 2000 called The Little Mermaid 2: Return to the Sea. The story revolves around Ariel's daughter and Ursula's evil sister, Morgana.

1770.   Mickey Mouse's head can be seen in Ursula's contract.

1771.   The film had a prequel in 2008 called The Little Mermaid: Ariel's Beginning.

1772.   The final scene took a year to animate. It was so difficult to draw, the animators had to rewatch the ocean scenes in Pinocchio to make the water's movements look right.

1773.   This was the first successful animated Disney film in decades. This began what is often known as the Disney Renaissance Era.

1774.   According to the producer, the final scene was inspired by Die Hard. I swear that's true.

1775.   The original fairy-tale is very different from the movie. In Hans Christian Anderson's version, the Mermaid (who has no name) makes a deal with a sea witch so she can walk on land. The sea witch agrees to this deal but only after cutting off the mermaid's tongue.

The witch also states that the Mermaid will turn into foam if the one she loves decides to marry anyone but her. Although the Mermaid is granted legs, it feels like she is walking on knives.

Although the prince falls for her, he decides to marry someone else. The Mermaid's sister tells her that she will return to being a Mermaid if she kills the prince with an enchanted blade. The Mermaid says she can't kill the one she loves and thus, jumps into the ocean, bursting into foam.

The Spirits of the Air are won over by her sacrifice and give her a soul so she can ascend to the afterlife...but only after she commits three centuries of good deeds. (Weirdly, doing tests for 300 years is a common theme in European folklore.)

The Lorax
2012

1776.   Danny DeVito voices the titular character. He also voices the character in German, Russian, Italian, and Spanish.

1777.   The story is based on Dr. Seuss' book of the same name. The 45-page book was published in 1971.

1778.   Zac Efron voices Ted. Ted is named after the original author. Dr. Seuss' real name was Theodore "Ted" Geisel.

1779.   Taylor Swift voices Audrey.

1780.   The film was released on Dr. Seuss' birthday, March 2nd.

1781.   The movie was criticized for warning children about corporate greed and yet it contained over 70 advertised products.

The Lord of the Rings
1978

1782.   This story focuses on the first two-thirds of the original novel. This film was supposed to have a sequel that covered the final third of the story. Sadly, the film bombed at the box office and the sequel was scrapped.

1783.   John Hurt voices Aragorn.

1784.   The film used an animation style called rotoscope. This required the crew to film actors in black-and-white and draw an animation cell over every frame.

1785.   The film was supposed to have Led Zeppelin songs but the director couldn't get the music rights.

1786.   The two main villains are Sauron and Saruman. The producers worried that the characters' names sounded too similar so they changed Saruman's name to "Aruman." Although this decision was reversed, Saruman is still referred to as "Aruman" several times.

1787.   Anthony Daniels voiced Legolas. Daniels is best-known for playing C-3P0 in the Star Wars films.

1788.   The director of the live-action Lord of the Rings, Peter Jackson, copied certain shots including when the Ringwraiths slash the beds to ribbons and when Frodo hides from the Ringwraiths.

1789.   The actors who voiced Frodo and Perry are brothers.

1790.   Orson Welles narrated the trailer.

1791.   Visionary director, Tim Burton, was one of the animators. It was his first job on a film.

Madagascar
2005

1792.   The film begins with a lion, a zebra, a giraffe and a hippo in Central Park Zoo. In real life, none of these animals are in this zoo.

1793.   Sacha Baron Cohen voices Julien. The character was supposed to have two lines. When Cohen improvised an eight-minute scene in an Indian accent, the filmmakers rewrote the script to accommodate his character. Julien plays a major role in all the Madagascar films.

1794.   Jada Pinkett Smith voices Gloria the hippo. Madonna was considered for the role.

1795.   Ben Stiller voices Alex the lion. While he is posing in the beginning, he performs the Blue Steel pose. This pose is from the film, Zoolander, which also starred Ben Stiller.

1796.   Melman the giraffe is so scared of getting ill, he wears tissue boxes on his feet. This is a reference to Howard Hughes who did the same thing due to his severe hypochondria.

Madagascar: Escape 2 Africa
2008

1797.   Ben Stiller voices Alex. Young Alex is played by Ben's son, Quinn.

1798.   Jada Pinkett Smith voices Gloria. Young Gloria is played by her daughter, Willow.

1799.   Bernie Mac voices Zuba. This film was dedicated to him as he died before the film was released.

1800.   Alec Baldwin voices Makunga the lion. Originally, Baldwin was going to play a caricature of himself.

1801.   The original subtitle was The Crate Escape.

1802.   All the zebras are voiced by Chris Rock.

1803.   Will.i.am voices Moto Moto.

1804.   An animated series called The Penguins of Madagascar was released the same year as this film.

1805.   The mark on Alex's paw is shaped like Africa. It even includes the island of Madagascar.

Madagascar: Europe's Most Wanted
2012

1806. Bryan Cranston voices Vitaly the tiger. Russel Brand and Kevin Spacey were considered for the role.

1807. Conrad Vernon directed the film. He voices Mason the monkey.

1808. Martin Short voices Stefano. Robin Williams, Jack Black, and Billy Crystal were considered for the role.

1809. Jessica Chastain voices Gia. Sigourney Weaver and Susan Sarandon were considered.

1810. Frances Mc Dormand voices Chaptain Chantal. Bette Midler and Carrie Fisher were considered.

1811. Vinnie Jones voices Freddie the dog.

Mary and Max
2009

1812.   One of the tombstones in the graveyard reads, "RIP Adam Elliot. Very over-rated. Elliott is the director."

1813.   This was the only film that Adam Elliot directed.

1814.   The story revolves around a girl called Mary who becomes pen pals with an autistic man called Max. According to the director, Max is based on "a pen-friend in New York who I've been writing to for over 20 years."

1815.   It took nine weeks to design and build the set.

1816.   It took over a year just to do principal photography for the film.

1817.   133 mini-sets, 212 puppets, and 475 props were made for the film.

<u>Meet the Robinsons</u>
2007

1818.   The story is based on the book, A Day with Wilbur Robinson.

1819.   The film was originally going to be live-action.

1820.   Jim Carrey was offered two roles but he turned them down to star in The Number 23.

1821.   Adam West voices Uncle Art.

1822.   There is a picture of Nikola Tesla in Lewis' wall in the orphanage.

1823.   The test-screening went so bad, 60% of the film had to be changed.

1824.   A picture of Walt Disney appears in the orphanage.

Megamind
2010

1825.   The film's plot was based on the premise, "What if Lex Luthor defeated Superman?"

1826.   Megamind's posters say, "No you can't." This is an obvious reference to Barack Obama's slogan, "Yes we can."

1827.   Ben Stiller voices Bernard. He auditioned for the titular role.

1828.   Will Ferrel voices Megamind. The studio's first choice for the role was Robert Downey Jr.

1829.   Megamind's lackey, Minion, is based on the alien in the film, Robot Monster.

1830.   Megamind's invisible car is a parody of Batman's Batmobile and Wonder Woman's Invisible Jet.

1831.   The original title was Master Mind.

1832.   Metro Man's poses are based on Elvis. Megamind's poses are based on Alice Cooper.

1833.   The film was supposed to be in live-action.

1834.   When Megamind confronts Metro Man, he says, "Speak, apparition." This line is taken from Hamlet.

1835.   Megamind mispronounces 20 words throughout the film.

Minions
2015

1836. The director voiced all 899 Minions.

1837. The Minion language is a mix of Hebrew, English, Spanish, German, French, Italian, Indonesian, Portuguese, and Malay.

1838. Sandra Bullock voices Scarlet Overkill. This is the first film where Sandra Bullock has played a villain.

1839. Sandra Bullock wore Minion-themed shoes for the premier.

1840. The film cost $74 million. The film made a staggering $1.15 billion at the box office. This was the first film to cost less than $100 million that grossed a billion dollars.

1841. The film mainly takes place in 1968. The Minions refer to this time as 42 BG (Before Gru.)

1842. The people in yellow jackets in the beginning shows what the Minions were supposed to look like in Despicable Me.

1843. There are 48 designs for the Minions.

1844. The cycloptic Minions are usually shorter than two-eyed Minions.

1845. The Minions accidentally killed Napoleon, Dracula, Genghis Khan, and the last T-Rex.

1846. A Minion will glow if it is shaken.

1847. The carpet in Herb's lab is the same carpet in the Overlook Hotel in The Shining.

1848. The Minions sometimes speak in perfect Indonesian. They say "terima kasih," which means "thank you," "kemari," which means "come here," and "yang mulia," which means "your highness."

1849.   Minions call apples "bapples."

1850.   One of the Minions usually says "sepala." Although this sounds like gibberish, he is actually saying "It's that way" in French and he uses it in the right context.

1851.   Flux is named after the flux capacitor from the film, Back to the Future.

1852.   The Minions are approximately one meter tall.

1853.   The crown is guarded by beefeaters. The beefeater on the left is modelled after former Prime Minister, David Cameron.

1854.   A young Gru can be seen at the VillainCon. He is watching Dr. Nefario using his freeze ray gun.

1855.   In the original script, the Minions were genetically altered corn kernels.

1856.   Minions say "bi-do," which means "I'm sorry."

1857.   When Scarlet asks the Minions if they know who Queen Elizabeth is, Kevin answers with, "La Cucaracha." This is Spanish for "Cockroach."

1858.   All the tall Minions have the same hairstyle.

1859.   The Minions are based on the Jawas from Star Wars and the Oompa Loompas from Willie Wonka and the Chocolate Factory.

1860.   In the first trailer, the Minions have crooked teeth. In the second trailer, the Minions have straight teeth.

1861.   Despite the fact that Scarlet's surname is Overkill, she doesn't kill anyone.

1862.   The villain from The Smurfs, Gargamel, is in front of the Minions at VillianCon.

Missing Link
2019

1863.   The film stars Hugh Jackman, Zoe Saldana, Stephen Fry, and Matt Lucas. Coincidentally, Hugh Jackman and Zoe Saldana both play Marvel characters. Also, Stephen Fry and Matt Lucas worked before on Alice in Wonderland.

1864.   Emma Thompson provides the voice of The Elder. David Walliams voices Lint. Stephen Fry voices Lord Piggot-Dunceby.

1865.   The film is in stop-motion. The bar scene required more shots than any stop-motion sequence ever.

1866.   The film was directed by Chris Butler, who also directed ParaNorman. This is the first film he's directed in seven years.

1867.   The story takes place in 1886.

1868.   Jack Blessing provides the voice of McVitie. This was the last film he starred in before he died.

1869.   The movie's fake title was Film Five.

1870.   The film was made by Cinerama. This was the first film they produced in 57 years.

1871.   This is the first film made by Laika where the main cast are adults.

1872.   Frost refers to Bigfoot as "Sasquatch" which means "hairy man."

1873.   The film concludes with Lionel Frost beginning his quest to track down the Feejee Mermaid. 19th century showman, PT Barnum, showcased the legendary Feejee Mermaid at his circus.
   In reality, the "mermaid" was composed of the upper body of a monkey sewn to the bottom of a fish.
   PT Barnum was played by Hugh Jackman in The Greatest Showman. By a freakish coincidence, Jackman voices Lionel Frost in this film.

Moana
2016

1874.   In many European countries, the title is Oceania and the main character is called Vianana. "Vianana" means "sheath."

1875.   The crab is called Tamatoa, which means "trophies."

1876.   There is a theory that Tamatoa is the reincarnation of Ursula, who is the main villain in The Little Mermaid.

1877.   The short, Inner Workings, was shown in the cinema before this film.

1878.   Jemaine Clement voices Tamatoa. Clement based the character on David Bowie.

1879.   Moana came out the same year as Zootopia. The last time Disney released two animated films in the same year was in 2002 when they released Lilo & Stitch and Treasure Planet.

1880.   Dwayne Johnson voices Muai. Johnson hates how animated films cast Hollywood actors for their star power rather than their talent and was worried that he was only cast because he is a celebrity. He kept checking with the director to make sure his performance was satisfactory.

1881.   Nicole Scherzinger voices Sina.

1882.   The genie's lamp can be seen on Tamatoa's shell.

1883.   Auli'I Cravalho voices Moana. She was the very last person to audition.

1884.   Cravalho never acted before she starred in this movie.

1885.   Cravalho turned 16 the day before the film's release. She is the youngest actress to portray a Disney princess.

1886.   At one point, a villager suggests cooking the chicken, Heihei. The chicken and the villager are voiced by the same actor, Alan Tudyk.

1887.   Heihei was supposed to be an intelligent animal. Ironically, he was changed into the dumbest character in Disney history.

1888.   Despite what viewers believe, the story doesn't take place in Hawaii. Instead, it takes place in Tonga, Fiji, and Samoa.

1889.   At one point, Maui turns into the Frozen character, Sven.

1890.   This is the first Disney princess movie where there is no love interest.

1891.   "Moana" means "blue."

1892.   Moana's pig is called Pua. "Pua" means "offspring."

1893.   Maui claims to have grabbed the Sun with his hook and lifted islands out of the sea. Maui performed these feats in Polynesian mythology.

1894.   Maui is the name of the second largest Hawaiian island.

1895.   The film has the same directors as Aladdin.

1896.   Moana's grandmother is called Tala. "Tala" means "story" in Samoan.

1897.   Disney looked at the cowboy film, True Grit, as an inspiration for the relationship between the two main characters.

1898.   When Maui fights, he performs a war dance called a Haka. The Maori people perform hakas before battle. Dwayne Johnson is of Maori descent.

1899.   When Maui meets Moana, he cocks his eyebrow. This is a signature move of Dwayne Johnson.

1900.   At one point, villagers can be seen beating a rug. If you look closely, you can see the rug looks the same as the magic carpet from Aladdin.

1901.   Maui's tattoos were not made with CGI. Instead, they were hand-drawn.

1902.   One of the Kakamora's is modelled on Baymax from Big Hero 6.

1903.   The film was originally going to revolve entirely around Maui. When the filmmakers ventured to Hawaii, they fell in love with the Polynesian folklore and thought the story would be better if a mortal character learned about the legend of Maui.

1904.   The Kakamora scene was inspired by the chase scene in Mad Max: Fury Road.

1905.   This is the second time that Dwayne Johnson has played a demi-god. He played the titular character in the film, Hercules.

Monsters, Inc.
2001

1906.   The short, For the Birds, was shown in the cinema before this film.

1907.   Mary Gibbs was only two-and-a-half when she voiced Boo. Pixar struggled getting Mary Gibbs to record her lines so they just followed her with a microphone. Whatever she said became her lines in the film.

1908.   The film has a lot of similarities to the 1989 film, Little Monsters. Both films revolves around a child who enters a monster's world from a portal in their bedroom and befriend a blue horned creature.

1909.   This was the first Pixar film where each character was designed by a different animator. This was done so each character would look as different as possible.

1910.   The film won an Oscar for Randy Newman's song, If I Didn't Have You.

1911.   The tagline was, "You Won't Believe Your Eye."

1912.   Frank Oz voices Funfus. Oz is best-known for puppeteering many monsters in the Star Wars series.

1913.   Mike tells Sulley that "You've been jealous of my good looks since the 4th grade." The prequel, Monsters University, shows that this is impossible since the two didn't meet until college.

1914.   The DVD comes with a short called Mike's New Car.

1915.   Boo's real name is Mary.

Monsters University
2013

1916.   The short, Blue Umbrella, was shown in the cinema before this film.

1917.   The School of Scaring building is a homage to Cthulhu. Cthulhu is the most famous character created by horror writer, HP Lovecraft.

1918.   Marcia Wallace voices the Librarian. Wallace is best-known for voicing Edna Krabappel in The Simpsons. She passed away four months after the film's release.

1919.   Alfred Molina voices Professor Knight. He's best-known for playing Doctor Octopus in Spider-Man 2.

1920.   In the first trailer, Slug has buck teeth.

1921.   Ariel's line from The Little Mermaid, "No Daddy, I love him!" can be heard during the Don't Scare the Teen scene.

1922.   In the original script, Mike and Sulley get trapped in the human world.

1923.   Although Helen Mirren was offered the role of Dean Hardscrabble, she insisted that she should audition to make sure she was right for the role.

Monsters vs. Aliens
2009

1924.   Most of the creatures are based on famous movie monsters. Reese Witherspoon's character, Ginormica, is based on the giant in Attack of the 50 Foot Woman. Hugh Laurie's character, Dr. Cockroach, is based on The Fly. Seth Rogen's character, BOB, is based on The Blob. Will Arnett's character, The Missing Link, is based on Creature from the Black Lagoon.

1925.   The tagline is, "The Weird Will Save the World."

1926.   The film revolves around the government using monsters for missions to take down hostile monsters. This concept is similar to the comic and movie, Hellboy. Weirdly, Jeffrey Tambor starred in both films.

1927.   Kiefer Sutherland voices WR Monger. His name is an obvious reference to the word, "warmonger."

1928.   WR Monger's insignia is based on Shrek's face.

1929.   This was the first animated film to be made in 3D. Every other film prior to this one was made in 2D and then converted into 3D.

1930.   The story is set in Modesto. This is the birthplace of George Lucas.

1931.   The song that the president plays on the synthesiser is the theme song from Beverly Hills Cop.

1932.   John Krasinksi voices Cuthbert. Ed Helms voices the News Reporter. Rainn Wilson voices the villain Gallaxhar. All these actors starred in the US version of The Office.

Mr. Peabody & Sherman
2014

1933.   Mr. Peabody originally appeared in the 1950s animated series, The Adventures of Rocky and Bullwinkle and Friends. His segments were known as Peabody's Improbably History.

1934.   Peabody is the world's smartest dog. He is so intelligent, he becomes bored with his life and decides to adopt a human child called Sherman. To entertain and educate Sherman, Peabody builds a time-machine and travels to pivotal moments in history.

1935.   Although Robert Downey Jr was cast as Peabody, he dropped out as he was too busy to commit to the role. Ty Burrell was then cast as Peabody.

1936.   The time-machine is called the WABAC, which is an abbreviation of Wavelength Acceleration Bi-directional Asynchronus Controller.

1937.   The WABAC travels at 88mph. This is the same speed the DeLorean travels in Back to the Future to travel through time.

1938.   The film spawned an animated series in 2015 called The Mr. Peabody & Sherman Show.

1939.   Peabody is an inventor, scientist, Nobel laureate, and a two-time Olympic medallist.

1940.   The film was supposed to come out in 2003.

1941.   The film was directed by Rob Minkoff. Minkoff directed The Lion King.

Mulan
1998

1942. Jackie Chan voices Shang in the Chinese version.

1943. Mulan is left-handed. This is a common trait in Disney characters that feel like they're different from everybody else.

1944. The film was nearly rated PG because of the use of the word, "cross-dresser."

1945. Mulan is credited for launching Christina Aguilera since her song, Reflection, was in the film.

1946. Chi Fu's name is Chinese for "bully."

1947. Mulan's name means "magnolia."

1948. Mulan is 16 years old.

1949. The Great Wall appears in the film even though it wasn't built until 600 years after the story is set.

1950. Lea Salonga provided Mulan's singing. She also sang as Jasmine in Aladdin.

1951. George Takei voices the First Ancestor.

1952. To capitalise on the success of the film, a rip-off came out the same year called The Secret of Mulan.

1953. Surprisingly, the film tanked in China. The Chinese found Mushu to be unbearably annoying. They also found the scene where the emperor bowed to Mulan incredibly disrespectful.

1954. Vice President, Mike Pence passionately hates this film because it depicts women being militaristic effective. That's right. He doesn't like a Disney cartoon (which has a talking dragon) because it's not believable.

Nausicaa of the Valley of the Wind
1984

1955.   This film was released in 1984. Shia LeBeouf (who was born in 1986) voices Asbel in the 2005 English dub. This means that Shia is credited for the film even though he wasn't born until after the film was originally released.

1956.   The film was heavily re-edited and released worldwide in 1985 as "Warriors of the Wind." The director, Hayao Miyazaki, was so upset about this cut that when a producer wanted to edit Miyazaki's film, Princess Mononoke, Miyazaki sent him a sword with the words, "NO CUTS" written on it.

1957.   Because it was directed by Miyazaki, many fans assume that this a Studio Ghibli film. However, the film was made before Studio Ghibli was formed.

1958.   Miyazaki was worried the film wouldn't sell because it wasn't based on any book or merchandise. To counter this, he created a comic based on the story to promote the film.

1959.   The military planes are based on the Nazi Luftwaffe.

1960.   The female is called Oh-Baba. Her name means "great old woman."

1961.   Nausicaa's glider is called Mehve. "Mehve" is German for "seagull."

1962.   The name "Nausicaa" comes from a character in Homer's The Odyssey.

The Nightmare Before Christmas
1993

1963.   Tim Burton came up with the story when he saw Halloween decorations being torn down from a shop and being replaced with Christmas decorations.

1964.   Tim Burton considered turning the story into a TV special.

1965.   Burton strongly considered making a sequel that revolved around St. Patrick's Day. The film would've been called The Unlucky Clover.

1966.   The lead character is Jack Skellington. He first appeared as an ornament in the film, Beetlejuice. Beetlejuice was directed by Tim Burton.

1967.   The shrunken head toy is a reference to the shrunken-headed man that appears in the final scene of Beetlejuice.

1968.   The snake that Jack delivers to kids looks exactly like the sandworm in the film, Beetlejuice.

1969.   The original story was a three-page poem. you can listen to Christopher Lee narrating the original poem on the DVD.

1970.   It took 100 people to make the film over a period of three years.

1971.   Behemoth is based on the B-movie actor and wrestler, Tor Johnson.

1972.   Sally's insides are made of leaves.

1973.   Because Sally has rigor mortis, the animators thought it'd be funny if she had trouble walking. This idea was scrapped as she looked drunk while walking.

1974.   Patrick Stewart was originally cast as the narrator.

1975.   Jack Skellington was supposed to have eyes.

1976.   Jack Skellington cameos as a pirate in the film, James and the Giant Peach.

1977.   Elvis-plates can be seen in the first house that Jack Skellington visits. This is a reference to Elvis' song, Blue Christmas.

1978.   Disney was worried The Nightmare Before Christmas was inappropriate for children so they dropped the film. It was then picked up by Touchstone Pictures. Weirdly, the trailer said that this was a Disney film even though it isn't.

1979.   Lock, Shock, and Barrel's names are derived from the phrase, "lock, stock, and barrel."

1980.   Paul Reubens voices Lock. Reubens is best-known for playing Pee Wee in the Pee Wee's Big Adventure.

1981.   There was a scene showing Oogie Boogie dancing with bugs but it was cut.

1982.   Stop-animation is so pain-staking, a character had be moved 12 times for one second of filming.

1983.   230 sets were made for the film.

1984.   There are seven Holiday Doors – Halloween, Christmas, Thanksgiving, Easter, St. Patrick's Day, Valentine's Day, and Independence Day.

1985.   Tim Burton made up the story when he was a teenager.

1986.   In the first draft, there were only three characters – Jack, Zero and Santa.

1987.   The scene where Jack reaches for the doorknob in Christmasland was the hardest shot to animate.

1988.   Danny Elfman composed the music for the film. He has composed several songs for Tim Burton films including the theme song for Beetlejuice and Batman.

1989.   Chris Sarandon voices Jack Skellington. When the producers learned that Sarandon couldn't sing, Danny Elfman was chosen to sing Skellington's songs.

1990.   Elfman also voices Barrel and Clown With The Tear Away Face.

1991.   Elfman said writing the songs for this film was "one of the easiest jobs I've ever had."

1992.   Zero's nose is a tiny jack-o-lantern.

1993.   In the opening scene, you can see that the bats are on wires. This movie is stop-motioned so the wires are completely unnecessary. They were put in as a reference to the awful special effects from old horror movies.

1994.   400 heads were made for Jack Skellington.

1995.   Vincent Price was cast as Santa Claus. Sadly, he died before he could complete his lines.

1996.   If a single frame was out of place, the animators had to reshoot an entire scene.

1997.   The film cost $18 million. It made $75 million at the box office.

1998.   The film was nearly made in 1982.

1999.   There are 60 characters in the film.

2000.   Up to four puppets were made for each character.

2001.   The director wanted Oogie Boogie to be Dr. Finklestein in disguise. Tim Burton was so angry when he heard this idea, he kicked a hole through a wall.

2002.   Despite the amount of effort that was put into the puppets, only four puppeteers worked on the film.

2003.   It took one week to film one minute of footage.

2004.   Two inventions were created for the film. The light alarm was devised to warn animators if the stage lights failed to come on. Also, a system was created so a puppeteer could switch to another puppet if their original puppet malfunctioned.

2005.   Despite what many people believe, this film was directed by Henry Selick, not Tim Burton. Burton was only on set for 10 days. Ironically, the film is called Tim Burton's The Nightmare Before Christmas in certain countries.

Oliver & Company
1988

2006.   The film was inspired by Oliver Twist.

2007.   Marlon Brando was considered for Sykes. He turned it down as he thought the film would bomb.

2008.   The tagline is, "The first Disney movie with attitude."

2009.   Whitney Houston was considered for Rita.

2010.   Oliver's name isn't mentioned until the last half hour of the movie.

2011.   Bette Midler voices Georgette.

2012.   Bill Joel voices Dodger. Steve Martin and Burt Rodgers were considered for the role.

2013.   Although this is one of the most obscure Disney animations, it did make a profit. It cost $31 million and made over $74 million at the box office.

Onward
2020

2014.   The story revolves around two elves who cast a spell to bring their deceased father back to life for one day. The director, Dan Scanlon was inspired to write this story since he lost his father at a young age.

2015.   Tom Holland provides the voice of Ian. Chris Pratt provides the voice of Barley. Both of them worked on Avengers: Infinity War and Avengers: Endgame.

2016.   This is the third film in three months where Tom Holland voices a character. He voices Walter in Spies in Disguise, Jip in The Voyage of Doctor Dolittle, and Ian in this film.

2017.   This is Pixar's first film that John Lasseter didn't work on. It is also the first Pixar film to be released in March.

2018.   This is the fifth Pixar film starring no humans.

Osmosis Jones
2001

2019.   William Shatner voices Mayor Phlegmming. The character is based on Richard Nixon.

2020.   Film director, Ron Howard, voices Tom Colonic. Colonic is based on JFK.

2021.   The tagline was, "He's one cell of a guy."

2022.   Kid Rock voices Kidney Rock.

2023.   The film stars Bill Murray and Chris Elliott. They worked together on Groundhog Day.

2024.   Laurence Fishburne voices Thrax.

2025.   In the year 2000, Warner Bros.' animation division was in financial jeopardy. For their first animated film of the 21st century, they had a choice to fund Brad Bird's film, The Incredibles, or Osmosis Jones.

When Warner Bros. chose Osmosis Jones, Brad Bird took his idea to Pixar and made one of the greatest animated films ever. The Incredibles made $633 million. By comparison, Osmosis Jones only made $14 million. This means that The Incredibles made 45 times more money than Osmosis Jones.

Unsurprisingly, the Warner Bros. Feature Animation department was shut down.

ParaNorman
2012

2026.   Mitch is the first openly gay character in an animated kids film. The movie received many complaints for depicting a gay character.

2027.   The tagline was, "It's all fun and games until someone raises the dead."

2028.   Casey Affleck voices Mitch.

2029.   Norman's ring tone is the Halloween theme song.

2030.   Anna Kendrick voices Courtney.

2031.   The faces of each character were created with 3D printers.

2032.   John Goodman voices Mr. Prenderghast. His name means "Ghost Holder."

2033.   The film was made with stop-motion instead of CGI. However, the stop-motion was so incredible, that people criticized the trailer, believing the animation was CGI.
        The studio had to release a second trailer showing how the characters were created to prove that the film was made with stop-motion, not CGI.

The Peanuts Movie
2015

2034.   The short, Cosmic Scrat-tastophy, was shown in cinemas before this film. The short revolves around Scrat from the Ice Age series.

2035.   This is the first Peanuts film in 35 years.

2036.   Despite what many people believe, Charlie Brown isn't bald. He has faded blond hair.

2037.   This is the first Peanuts film since the death of its creator, Charles M. Schulz. He passed away in 2000.

2038.   The trees never sway. This was done to emulate the same look as the original comic strip.

2039.   The film is called Snoopy and Charlie Brown in most countries.

2040.   The tagline was, "The story of an underdog. And his dog."

2041.   It took nine years to make this film.

2042.   The film was released 65 years after the first Peanuts comic strip.

2043.   Charlie Brown's book report is on War and Peace. This was the writer's favourite novel.

Penguins of Madagascar
2016

2044. Benedict Cumberbatch voices Classified. He had great difficulty pronouncing "penguins." He kept saying "pengwings."

2045. Dave the Octopus disguises himself as a human called Dr. Octavious Brine. This is a reference to the Spider-Man supervillain, Doctor Octopus.

2046. Renowned director, Werner Herzog, voices the documentary filmmaker.

2047. All of Dave's orders to the octopuses refer to a celebrity.
   i)   "Drew! Barry! More power!" – Drew Barrymore
   ii)   "Charlize, they're on the ray!" – Charlize Theron
   iii)   "Nicholas! Cage them!" – Nicholas Cage
   iv)   "Halle, bury them." – Halle Berry
   v)   "Hugh, Jack, man the battle station." – Hugh Jackman
   vi)   "William, hurt them." – William Hurt
   vii)   "Helen, hunt them down." – Helen Hunt
   viii) "Robin, write this down." – Robin Wright
   ix)   "Kevin, bake on." – Kevin Bacon
   x)   "Elijah, would you please take them away." – Elijah Wood

Peter Pan
1953

2048.   Many sources state that the name, Wendy, first appeared in the original play of Peter Pan. This isn't true.

2049.   There is a theory that Captain Hook killed Ariel's mother. Ariel is the main character in The Little Mermaid.

2050.   In the play, Hook and Mr. Darling are usually played by the same actor. In this film, Hans Conried voices both roles.

2051.   In the play, the dog and the crocodile are played by the same actor. To reference this, the animators made the crocodile have canine-like attributes.

2052.   Walt Disney played Peter Pan in a play.

2053.   This is Michael Jackson's favourite film.

2054.   Walt Disney tried to buy the rights for this story in 1935.

2055.   At one point, the story was going to be told from Nana's viewpoint.

2056.   Although many sources state that Marilyn Monroe was the inspiration for Tinkerbell, this isn't true. Margaret Kerry was the model for the character. She voices the red-headed mermaid.

2057.   The nine original creators of Snow White and the Seven Dwarfs were nicknamed the Nine Old Men. This is the last animated Disney film that they worked on.

2058.   Bill Thompson voices Smee. He voices the White Rabbit in Alice in Wonderland.

2059.   The film cost $4 million. It made $87 million at the box office.

2060.   Originally, Nana the dog was supposed to travel to Neverland.

2061.   The sequel, Return to Neverland, was released in 2002. It is one of the few animated Disney films that received a cinematic release.

2062.   Bobby Driscoll voices the titular role. He was the first male to play Peter Pan in a film.

2063.   Katheryn Beaumont voices Wendy. Beaumont voices the titular character in Alice in Wonderland.

2064.   Peter Pan is named after the Greek god of the wild, Pan. Pan plays a wind-instrument, much like Peter Pan.

2065.   Walt Disney was disappointed with this film because he found Peter Pan cold and unlikeable.
         Experts on the original story said that Pan was portrayed perfectly as he was originally written as selfish and ruthless. When the Lost Boys grow too old in the play, Peter begins "thinning out" their numbers. Many readers believe this means that Peter either abandons or kills the Lost Boys when they grow too old.

Pinocchio
1940

2066.   The film is based on the 1883 story, The Adventures of Pinocchio, which was written by Carlo Collodi.

2067.   In the original story, Pinocchio's nose grew when he got stressed and not necessarily when he lied.

2068.   In the book, the cricket is simply called The Talking Cricket.

2069.   In the book, Pinocchio kills the Talking Cricket with a hammer.

2070.   In the film, the Fox and the Cat rob Pinocchio. In the book, they hang him.

2071.   In the film, Geppetto and Pinocchio get attacked by a whale. In the book, they get swallowed by a sea monster called the Terrible Dogfish.

2072.   "Pinocchio's" name is derived from the word "pinolo", which means "pine seed."

2073.   Evelyn Venable provided the voice and physical model for the Blue Fairy. She was also the model for the Colombia Studios logo.

2074.   Honest John coaxes Pinocchio to Pleasure Island with the ace of spades, calling it his "ticket." Tarot readers refer to the ace of spades as The Death Card.

2075.   Honest John's real name is John Worthington Foulfellow.

2076.   The original budget was $500,000. It ballooned to $2.6 million. The film flopped because it came out during World War II.

2077.   When Walt Disney picked up his Oscar for Snow White and the Seven Dwarfs, he talked about a new film he was working on for 25 minutes. That film was Pinocchio.

2078.   The film was in production for nine months before Walt Disney inserted Jiminy Cricket into the story.

2079.   Walt Disney shut down production at one point to rethink the story and redesign some of the characters.

2080.   The film wasn't released in Germany or Japan until the 1950s because of World War II.

2081.   Mel Blanc voices Figaro, Gideon, and the Donkeys. Blanc is best-known for voicing Bugs Bunny.

2082.   When Pinocchio is a wooden boy, he has three fingers. When he is turned into a real boy, he has four fingers.

2083.   Figaro the cat is Walt Disney's favourite character in the film.

The Pirates!
Band of Misfits
2012

2084.   The plague ship was originally called the leper ship but the word "leper" was removed after a leprosy charity complained.

2085.   Most of the main cast is British. Many of the actors were replaced with Americans when the film was released in the US.

2086.   The original title was The Pirates! In an Adventure with Scientists! This is the title of the 2004 book that the film is based on.

2087.   The Irish pirate wears a Blue Peter badge.

2088.   The film inspired a short called So You Want to Be a Pirate!

2089.   The Elephant Man appears for a second in the scene where the Pirate Captain is selling baby clothes.

2090.   David Tennant voices Charles Darwin. Darwin meets Queen Victoria in this film. Weirdly, Tennant's character also met Queen Victoria in Doctor Who.

2091.   Although the film was made with stop-motion, CGI was used for the sky and sea.

2092.   Since the story is set in 1837, Queen Victoria should be 17.

Pocahontas
1995

2093.　Only two animated Disney films are based on a true story; this and Mulan.

2094.　The tree, Grandmother Willow, was originally going to be a male called Old Man River.

2095.　The film was in production for five years.

2096.　Christian Bale voices Thomas. He plays Rolfe in The New World, which revolved around Pocahontas.

2097.　Some crew-members of The Lion King abandoned the film and decided to work on Pocahontas instead, believing it was going to be more successful. Ironically, The Lion King made over $900 million.

2098.　55 animators designed the Pocahontas character.

2099.　The film premiered in Central Park. Disney representatives worried that it might rain while the film was being shown. Weirdly, it only rained during a raining scene in the film.

2100.　Stephen Fry was considered for the role of Governor Ratcliffe. The role went to David Ogden Stiers, who voiced Cogsworth in Beauty and the Beast.

2101.　In real life, Pocahontas was called Matoaka. Her people nicknamed her "Pocahontas" which means "frisky." She was 13 when the Settlers arrived and she often ran around them topless.

She was never in love with John Smith and instead, married another settler called John Rolfe when she was 18 and had a child called Thomas. She converted to Christianity and took on the name, Rebecca.

She moved to England with Rolfe in 1617 when she was 21. Sadly, she died the same year from unknown causes.

2102.   Irene Bredard voices Pocahontas. Of the 60+ actresses that have portrayed her over the years, Bredard is one of the only people who is Native American. She is part Eskimo and part Cree Indian. She went on to play Pocahontas' mother in the 2005 film, The New World.

2103.   Pocahontas' tribe are called Powhatan (also known as Powatan.)

2104.   Originally, all the animals could speak. Their dialogue was cut to make the tone more serious.

2105.   Pocahontas uses willow bark on John Smith after he is shot. Willow bark contains salicylic acid, which is a fundamental component in aspirin.

2106.   The writers considered having Pocahontas' people only speak in Powhatan.

2107.   Billy Connolly voices Ben.

2108.   John Candy was cast as Redfeather the turkey. Although he had most of his voiceover work done, the character was scrapped when Candy suddenly died.

2109.   Pocahontas is American. The only other American Disney princess is Tiana from the 2009 film, The Princess and the Frog.

2110.   Pocahontas is 18 years old.

2111.   Colours of the Wind won an Oscar for Best Song. The film won another Oscar for Best Music Score.

2112.   Sean Bean was considered for John Smith. The role went to Mel Gibson.

2113.   This was the first animated Disney film to have an interracial romance.

2114.   The film was released on June 23rd 1995. This was the 400th anniversary of Pocahontas's birth.

2115. Jeffrey Katzenberg was the studio head of Disney at the time of this film's release. He was so proud of Pocahontas that he thought it would be Oscar-nominated for Best Film. The film was panned and it didn't make as much money as Disney expected.

2116. Many sources say this film is a flop which it isn't true. It cost $55 million and made $346 million at the box office.

2117. The story has many similarities to Moana. Both stories revolve around a young woman who is expected to rule the land against her wishes. Both characters are content roaming through their land and sing about the beauty of their home (especially the water.) Pocahontas and Moana seek counsel from a mysterious elderly female who tells her that there is a conflict beyond the sea which will lead to her destiny.

They then encounter a gold-obsessed villain and a cocky, chauvinist who eventually becomes an ally. To prove herself to her new ally, both heroines overestimate their abilities and nearly get their ally killed.

Doubting her abilities, Moana/Pocahontas's spirit guide gives her a pep talk and they decide to end the conflict through love rather than violence. Both characters then become the leader and usher in a new age of hope.

Pokémon: The First Movie
Mewtwo Strikes Back
1998

2118.   This film had the highest-grossing opening for an animated film in history. However, the film lost that title two weeks later to Toy Story 2.

2119.   Since Mewtwo is psychic, he doesn't speak since he can project his thoughts into people's minds. The animators were relieved by this since they had great difficulty matching up the lip movements of each character when they spoke.

2120.   The Japanese version has a completely different story.

2121.   Dragonite has a purse. The director joked that he hoped this would make male purses come back in style.

2122.   In the Japanese version, Mewtwo is perceived in a more sympathetic light since he sees himself as an outsider who simply wants to belong in the world. In the American version, Mewtwo is an evil tyrant who wishes to control the world.

2123.   This story was originally going to be the finale for the animated series.

2124.   The main characters make a huge speech at the end explaining how "fighting is wrong." Many fans found this speech illogical since the entire premise of Pokémon is to battle each other. Every single episode of the Pokémon animated series has a Pokémon battle.

2125.   The film spawned over 20 sequels.

The Prince of Egypt
1998

2126.　　Val Kilmer voices God and Moses. This is a reference to the film, The Ten Commandments, where Charlton Heston plays both characters.

2127.　　Christian Bale plays Moses in the 2014 film, Exodus: Gods and Kings. Weirdly, Bale also succeeded Val Kilmer as Batman.

2128.　　Despite the fact the filmmakers consulted with 600 religious experts to make the story authentic, there are many differences between this film and the Biblical account of Exodus.
i)　　In the film, Moses kills a slave master by accident. In the Bible, Moses murdered the man and then tried to hide the body.
ii)　　In the Bible, Moses is adopted by the Pharaoh's wife, not his daughter.
iii)　　In the Bible, Aaron turned the staff into a snake, not Moses.
iv)　　In the Bible, Aaron turned the water of the Nile into blood, not Moses.

2129.　　Steven Martin, Ralph Fiennes, Michelle Pfeiffer, and Martin Short performed their own singing.

2130.　　Sandra Bullock voices Miriam. Jeff Goldblum voices Aaron. Patrick Stewart voices Seti.

2131.　　Ofra Haza voices Yocheved. Of the 20 languages the film was dubbed in, Haza dubbed 17 of them herself. Helen Mirren voices the Queen.

2132.　　The film takes place in 1200 BC.

2133.　　At the time, it was the most expensive animated film ever, costing $70 million. It made over $218 million at the box office.

2134.　　This was co-directed by Brenda Chapman. She was the first female to a major animated feature. She also co-directed the film, Brave.

2135.　　The song, When You Believe, won an Oscar.

2136.   The film was sent to theatres under the codename "Edgar Allen. This name is based on the poet, Edgar Allen Poe. "POE" is the initials of "Prince of Egypt."

2137.   A shadow can be seen in the Red Sea after it has risen. Many viewers assume the shadow is of a whale. It is actually of a Megalodon shark; the largest shark to ever exist.

2138.   This film was banned in Malaysia and Indonesia.

2139.   The Red Sea parting scene required ten animators and took two years to animate.

2140.   The final plague kills every firstborn child apart from those who have marked their doors with lamb's blood.
        The constellation of Orion is visible when the final plague takes place. Orion was a gigantic huntsman in Greek mythology who hunted for his god, Zeus. This constellation seems applicable to the scene as a godly spirit is hunting down the first-born children.

The Princess and the Frog
2009

2141.   The original title was The Frog Princess.

2142.   There is a rip-off of The Princess and the Frog (which is unimaginatively called The Frog Prince.) It was released days before this film.

2143.   Tiana was originally called Maddy.

2144.   Anika Noni Rose voices Tiana. Beyoncé, Jennifer Hudson, Alicia Keys, and Tyra Banks were considered for the role.

2145.   Dr. Facilier's face is based on the Voodoo god of magic. His chipped tooth is based on his voice actor, Keith David.

2146.   Oprah Winfrey voices Eudora.

2147.   After the Disney film, The Princess and the Frog, was released, there were dozens of reports of children being hospitalized with salmonella after kissing frogs.

2148.   This was Disney's first fairy tale since Aladdin.

2149.   The prince is called Naveen. "Naveen" is Indian for "new."

2150.   Nobody calls Dr. Facilier by his real name apart from himself. Everyone else calls him the Shadow Man.

2151.   This was the first 2D Disney film where all the voice actors performed their own singing since Beauty and the Beast.

Princess Mononoke
1997

2152.   Until the release of Spirited Away, this was considered to be the greatest anime ever.

2153.   The film's director, Hayao Miyazaki, started writing the story in the 1970s.

2154.   The princess is called San, not Mononoke. This is confusing because the title is a half-translation. "Mononoke" means "vengeful spirit."

2155.   The film was made of 144,000 animation cells. It is the last major animated film to be filmed on plastic animation cels. Some sources state that Hayao Miyazaki personally drew half of these but he has dismissed this.

2156.   Hayao Miyazaki said if he wasn't allowed to make this film, he would've made a film about caterpillars.

2157.   This was supposed to be the director's final film. It became so successful that he has made several films since.

Puss in Boots
2011

2158.   Antonio Banderas voices Puss. To advertise the film, he posted many pictures of himself at screenings surrounded by cats.

2159.   The animators didn't need to bring in cats to study for Puss' movements. Instead, they studied cat videos on YouTube.

2160.   The tagline is, "Looking good never looked so good."

2161.   Zach Galifiankis voices the villain, Humpty Alexander Dumpty.

2162.   The film had an animated spin-off called The Adventures of Puss in Boots. The show premiered in 2015 and ran for 50 episodes.

2163.   Salma Hayek voices Kitty Softpaws. This is the fifth time Hayek has worked with Banderas.

2164.   Puss says, "Holy frijoles." "Frioles" means "beans."

2165.   The film is called Cat in Boots in United Arab Emirates.

Ralph Breaks the Internet
2018

2166.   All the Disney Princesses star in this film. Mary Costa is the only living voice actress not to reprise her role as a Disney Princess, Aurora. Since Costa is 88, her voice wouldn't be suitable to play the 16-year-old character.

2167.   In Germany, the title translates into Webcrasher. In Argentina, it's called Wifi Ralph. In Portugal, it's called Ralph vs Internet.

2168.   The film takes place six years after the previous one.

2169.   Nicole Scherzinger voices Mo's Mom.

2170.   Alan Tudyk provides the voice of Knowmore. This is the sixth animated Disney film that Tudyk has starred in. He plays King Candy in Wreck-It Ralph, the Duke in Frozen, Alistair in Big Hero 6, Weaselton in Zootropolis, and Heihei in Moana.

2171.   Phil Johnson is the director and he provides the voice of the Surge Protector. This is the first film he ever directed.

2172.   The film was released one day before the 18th birthday of Auli'I Cravalho, who provides the voice of Moana. Moana was released one day before her 16th birthday.

2173.   The film was delayed by a year so Disney could focus on Zootropolis.

2174.   This film came out two years after Moana. This is the longest gap between two animated Disney films since The Great Mouse Detective in 1986 and Oliver & Company in 1988.

2175.   There was supposed to be a joke about the Star Wars villain, Kylo Ren, being a spoilt brat but Disney rejected it.

2176.   Stan Lee cameos just before Vanellope meets the Disney princesses.

2177.   Vin Diesel cameos as Baby Groot.

2178.   Bill Hader voices JP Spamley.

2179.   The Disney Princesses in the film are Belle, Merida, Mulan, Anna, Elsa, Rapunzel, Ariel, Pocahontas, Jasmine, Snow White, Tiana, and Cinderella.

Weirdly, Esmeralda from The Hunchback of Notre Dame is absent from the line-up. Although you could argue she is absent because she is not a princess, neither is Anna or Moana.

Although Elsa was a princess in Frozen, she became a queen when her parents died.

2180.   The Disney princesses' shirts' reads something that references their personality. Moana's shirt reads, "#SHINY" with a picture of Tamatoa the crab. Elsa's shirt reads, "Just Let It Go." Ariel's shirt reads, "Gizmos & Whooz-its & that's-its & Snarfblats & Dinglehoppers." Aurora's shirt reads "Nap Queen." Anna's shirt reads, "Finish Each Other's." Snow White's shirt reads, "Poison." Merida's shirt reads "Mum" and has a picture of a bear. Belle's shirt reads "BFF. Beast Friends Forever." Jasmine's shirt reads, "Three Wishes." Cinderella's shirt reads "G2G."

2181.   Ralph and Vanellope were meant to meet the Disney princesses in the video game, Disney Infinity.

2182.   Mindy Kaling is the only actor to appear in the previous film that was recast for Ralph Breaks the Internet. Although she played Taffyta in Wreck-It Ralph, she was replaced with Melissa Villasenor. It is unknown what Kaling didn't return for the role.

2183.   The video game, Slaughter Race, is based on the 1995 franchise, Twisted Metal.

2184.   Gal Gadot voices Shank. The character is based on the Fast and the Furious character, Gisele, who Gadot also played.

2185.   Litwak's Arcade is situated in Los Aburridos. "Aburrido" is Spanish for "boring."

2186.   When Ralph enters the OlderNet, he crosses a Y2K survival kit.

2187.   The end-credits are 13 minutes long.

2188.   The film received criticism as Moana's skin colour appears lighter than in her original film.

2189.   The film cost $175 million. It made $526 million at the box office.

2190.   One of the Stormtroopers from Star Wars performs a Wilhelm Scream. This sound effect is used in every Star Wars film and is the most famous scream in movie history.

2191.   Weirdly, this film and the previous one came out the same year as a Dr. Seuss adaptation. Wreck-It Ralph came out the same year as The Lorax. This film came out the same year as The Grinch.

Ratatouille
2007

2192.   The short, Lifted, was shown before this film in the cinema.

2193.   To save money, no human characters have toes.

2194.   Hair is the hardest thing to animate so Remy was exceptionally difficult to create. For a human, 110,000 hairs have to be animated. For Remy, 1.15 million hairs had to be animated.

2195.   Marketing tie-ins for the film were difficult because no food company wanted to associate with a rat.

2196.   During productions, the animators had pet rats for a year so they could study their movements.

2197.   If you look closely, you can see that the chefs have scratches and burn marks on their wrists, just like real chefs.

2198.   There is a rip-off of Ratatouille called Ratatoing. It is also a rip-off of Mission Impossible...for some reason.

2199.   Pixar was afraid no one would know how to pronounce Ratatouille so the phonetic pronunciation was on all posters and trailers.

2200.   Anton Ego writes his review in a room shaped like a coffin.

2201.   At one point, the Head Chef gets wet. To animate this shot realistically, the animators dressed up a crewmember in a chef outfit and put him in a swimming pool to see which parts of his outfit stuck to his body and which parts were see-through.

2202.   Remy's ratatouille is called confit byaldi.

2203.   The director intentionally made female animators draw female characters as much as possible.

2204.   Originally, a large section of the story was going to take place underground.

2205.   The French waiter who talks about cheese is voiced by the director, Brad Bird.

2206.   The story was pitched by Jan Pinkava in 2001. Disney believed Pinkava wasn't good enough for the project and had him replaced with Brad Bird in 2005.

2207.   Ratatouille received five Oscar nominations. At the time of the film's release, this was the most Oscar nominations an animated film ever received.

2208.   The DVD includes the short, Your Friend the Rat.

2209.   Because Joe Ranft died in 2006, this was the first Pixar film that he didn't star in.

2210.   Auguste Gusteau's name means "scent lord."

2211.   Auguste Gusteau's first name is an anagram of his surname.

The Rescuers
1977

2212. Despite the fact that Walt Disney died 11 years before the film's release, he had a lot of input in the story because he began working on it in 1962. He died four years later.

2213. Eva Gabor voices Bianca. She voiced the lead character, Bianca, in The AristoCats.

2214. Medusa's pet alligators are called Brutus and Nero.

2215. Upon its release, some viewers complained that the film's art looked lazy and sketchy. This art technique was intentional and was also used for The Sword in the Stone.

2216. A Mickey Mouse watch appears on the wall of the Rescue Aid Society building.

2217. Although the owl's name is never mentioned, he is called Deacon.

2218. The rabbit is called Deadeye.

2219. The albatross is called Orville. He is named after Orville Wright, who invented the first plane with his brother, Wilbur.

2220. Penny freezes every time she looks at Madame Medusa. This is a reference to the Greek mythological creature, Medusa the Gorgon, who turned people to stone with her gaze.

Rescuers Down Under
1990

2221. This was the first animated Disney sequel.

2222. George C. Scott voices McLeach. Clint Eastwood was considered for the role.

2223. John Candy voices Wilbur. Dan Aykroyd was considered for the role.

2224. Cody is derived from the Irish word "cuidigtheach" which means "guardian."

2225. Douglas Seale voices Krebbs. Seale voices the Sultan in Aladdin.

2226. The Prince and the Pauper was shown in cinemas before this film.

2227. There are no songs in the film.

2228. The film cost $30 million. The film made less than $28 million at the box office. As a result, Disney didn't release a theatrical sequel for an animated film for years.

Rio
2011

2229.   Will.i.am voices Pedro.

2230.   The tagline is, "1 out of every 8 Americans is afraid of flying. Most of them don't have feathers."

2231.   Pixar cancelled their film, Newt, because the story was too similar to Rio.

2232.   Jesse Eisenberg voices the lead character, Blu. He recorded his lines during the weekends.
    During the weekdays, he worked on The Social Network. Eisenberg agreed to star in Rio as he thought it would be fun compared to The Social Network which he considered a "joyless" experience.

2233.   When Tulio sees his reflection while he is dressed as a macaw, he says, "Cyanopsitta Spixxi!" This is the scientific name for the Spix's macaw.

Rise of the Guardians
2012

2234.   Santa Claus is depicted as a Russian called North. Every time he is surprised, North shouts the name of a classic Russian composter like Shostakovich or Rimsky-Korsakov.

2235.   The film revolves around a league of fairy tale characters like Santa, the Easter Bunny, the Sandman, Jack Frost, and the Tooth Fairy. If the film did well, the director expected to make sequels with many more mythical characters. Sadly, the film only made a minor profit and the series was cancelled.

2236.   Chris Pine voices Jack Frost. The role was supposed to go to Leonardo DiCaprio.

2237.   Jack Frost calls the Easter Bunny a kangaroo. This is because Bunny's voice actor, Hugh Jackman, is Australian.

Road to El Dorado
2000

2238.   The film cost $95 million. It only made $76 million at the box office. This was the only animated film that DreamWorks made that didn't earn its money back.

2239.   The armadillo is called Bibo.

2240.   The sacred book shows a picture of a man fishing from the moon. This is a parody of DreamWorks' logo.

2241.   The Spanish general is called Cortes. In real life, his name was Gonzalo Pizarro.

2242.   Antonio Banderas turned down the lead role, Tulio. The role went to Kevin Kline.

2243.   Kevin Kline and Kenneth Branagh voice the main characters. They worked together in Wild Wild West.

2244.   The original title was City of Gold.

2245.   The film was based on Rudyard Kipling's story, The Man Who Would Be King.

2246.   The game that Tulio and Miguel play with the Aztecs is called Tlachtli. The way this game is portrayed in the film is surprisingly accurate. The players had to knock the 9lb ball into the hoop using their hips. The team only had to score one point to win the game.
        The game was so hard, the teams could play all day without scoring a single point. The captain of the losing team would be beheaded. Sometimes, the entire losing team would be sacrificed.

Robin Hood
1973

2247.   Friar Tuck was originally going to be a pig instead of a badger.

2248.   Five of the actors were in The AristoCats.

2249.   Phil Harris voices Little John. He voices Baloo in The Jungle Book and O' Malley in The AristoCats.

2250.   This film started as the European fable, Reynard the Fox.

2251.   Terry Jones from the Monty Python series was considered for the titular role.

2252.   Marge Champion modelled for Maid Marion. She also modelled for the titular character in Snow White and the Seven Dwarfs and Duchess in The AristoCats.

2253.   To save money and time, the dancing in the woods scenes was copied frame-by-frame from the dance scenes in Snow White and the Seven Dwarfs, The AristoCats, and The Jungle Book.

Robots
2005

2254.   Robots was directed by Chris Wedge. He is most famous for voicing Scrat from the Ice Ages series.

2255.   Robin Williams voices Fender. If Robin Williams had to do a scene ten times, he would usually try it in ten different accents.

2256.   Paula Abdul voices Watch.

2257.   Jim Broadbent voices the villain, Madame Gasket.

2258.   The tagline was, "Repair for adventure!"

2259.   This was the first animated film that Robin Williams starred in since Aladdin and the King of Thieves.

2260.   This was originally going to be a musical.

2261.   On Fender's Map of the Stars Homes, it reads – Jeremy Iron, Orson Wheels, Axle Roses, Britney Gears, Farrah Faucet, and MC Hammer.

Sausage Party
2016

2262.   The film's creator, Seth Rogen, concocted the idea when he noticed how Disney and Pixar were humanizing everything (cars, toys, insects, robots, etc.) and he wondered what would be the weirdest thing you could humanize.

He believed the most messed up thing a person could project their emotions onto is food since its purpose is to be eaten. He realised that a film about this concept would be horrifying but hilarious.

2263.   The film is rated R for its vulgar language, violent images, and lude characters. The trailer was accidentally shown before a screening of Finding Dory, which left children horrified.

2264.   Edward Norton voices Sammy. He based the character on Woody Allen.

2265.   The main characters in the film are not sausages. They are frankfurters.

2266.   The film was directed by Greg Tiernan. Before making this film, the only thing he directed was Thomas the Tank adaptions.

2267.   The film only cost $19 million. It made $140 million, making it the most successful R-rated animated film ever.

2268.   The film was in production for six years.

2269.   Sean "Diddy" Combs was meant to play a hot dog. Diddy changed his mind when he learned the film was animated.

2270.   Salma Hayek voices Teresa. She improvised the line, "Once you go taco, you never go back-o."

2271.   The movie only cost $19 million because the producers cut every corner possible. Many of the animators were forced to work overtime without pay. If animators refused to work extra time, they were fired. A lot of the animators' names were not included in the credits.

Scoob
2020

2272.   Zac Efron provides the voice of Fred. Dwayne Johnson was considered for the role.

2273.   This is the first time since 1988 where Frank Welker doesn't provide the voice for Fred. However, Welker does reprise the role of Scooby.

2274.   Scooby Doo is one of the most iconic cartoons made by Hanna-Barbera, who also made The Jetsons, Wacky Races, The Flintstones, Captain Caveman, and many others. This film is meant to be the first instalment of the Hanna-Barbera Cinematic Universe.

2275.   Mark Wahlberg provides the voice of Blue Falcon. Scoob is his first animated film.

2276.   Will Forte provides the voice of Shaggy. This is the first time in 11 years where the character was not voiced or portrayed by Matthew Lillard. Jason Lee, Jack Black, and Bill Hader were considered.

2277.   Gina Rodriguez provides the voice of Velma Dinkley. Awkwafina was considered for the role.

2278.   Amanda Seyfried provides the voice of Daphne. Anna Kendrick, Karen Gillan, and Bryce Dallas Howard were considered.

2279.   Shaggy's real name is Norville.

The Secret Life of Pets
2016

2280.   Gru from Despicable Me can be seen in the park in the beginning scene.

2281.   Louie CK voices the main character, Max.

2282.   The animators watched tons of funny animal videos on YouTube and incorporated the animals' movements into the film.

2283.   The filmmakers told funny stories to each other that revolved around their pets. The animators then incorporated as many of these stories into the film as possible.

2284.   The leader of the Flushed Pets is called Snowball. Snowball hates humans because they mistreated him. This is a reference to the book, Animal Farm, where a pig called Snowball leads a revolt against humans.

2285.   Kevin Hart voices Snowball.

2286.   Albert Brooks voices Tiberius the hawk. He is best-known for voicing Marlin in Finding Nemo.

2287.   Steven Coogan voices Ozone.

2288.   When Max and Duke flee from the Flushed Pets, a turtle starts knocking into animals. While it collides into the animals, it makes the same sound effect from Super Mario Bros. when a Koopa Troopa crashes into other enemies.

The Secret Life of Pets 2
2019

2289.   Harrison Ford provides the voice of Rooster. This is the first animated film he has starred in.

2290.   The tagline is, "With great power comes great adorability." This line is a parody of the Spider-Man line, "With great power comes great responsibility." Coincidentally, the film came out a month early so it wouldn't compete against Spider-Man: Far From Home.

2291.   The white tiger is called Hu. "Hu" is Mandarin for "tiger."

2292.   By a freakish coincidence, this is the second time a Secret Life of Pets film came out the same year that Jon Favreau directed a live-action reboot of a Disney film. He directed The Jungle Book in 2016 and he directed The Lion King in 2019.
   Also, both Secret Life of Pets films came out the same year as an Angry Birds film.

2293.   Louie CK provided the voice of Max in the previous film. After it was revealed that Louie CK had been sexually inappropriate towards women, he was replaced with Patton Oswalt.
   Jack Black, Bill Hader, Ashton Kutcher, Andy Samberg, Chris Pratt, and Jason Lee were considered for the role.

The Secret of NIMH
1982

2294.   The film is based on the novel, Mrs. Frisby and the Rats of NIMH. It was written by Robert C. O'Brien in 1971.

2295.   In the novel, the main character is called Brisby, not Frisby. Her name was changed to avoid legal ramifications from the Frisbee company, Wham-O.

2296.   The director was Don Bluth. He left Disney to make this film. It was rejected by Disney for being "too dark." After it did well, 20 Disney animators left the company. They were known as the Disney Defectors.

2297.   The dragonfly that Mr. Ages chases is Evinrude; the same dragonfly from The Rescuers.

2298.   Renowned thespian, Derek Jacobi, voices Nicodemus.

2299.   Will Wheaton voices Martin. This was his film debut. He is best-known for playing Wesley in Star Trek: The Next Generation.

2300.   The sword fight at the end was almost entirely copied from the climactic scene in The Adventures of Robin Hood.

2301.   The film cost $7 million. At the time, this was the most expensive animated film that was not made by Disney.

2302.   The film has many supernatural elements. These aspects do not exist in the original novel.

Shark Tale
2004

2303.   Many of the products have a fish-pun name e.g. Coral Cola (Coca-Cola,) Newsreef (Newsweek,) Old Wavy (Old Navy,) Gup (GAP,) etc.

2304.   The title was going to be Sharkslayer but the CEO changed it at the last minute, worried that it sounded too scary.

2305.   Ziggy Marley voices Ernie the Jellyfish. Ziggy is Bob Marley's son.

2306.   Will Smith voices Oscar. The animators made Oscar's ears stick out like Smith's do in real life.

2307.   When Oscar goes to the clock, there's a note on the wall that reads, "If you don't come in Saturday, don't bother." The CEO, Jeffrey Katzenberg, infamously sent this memo to executives while he was in charge of Disney.

2308.   The story is very similar to the 1897 tale, The Reluctant Dragon, which was written by Kenneth Grahame. Grahame is best-known for writing The Wind in the Willows.

2309.   Robert De Niro voices Don Lino. Like De Niro, Don Lino has a mole on his cheek.

Shaun the Sheep Movie
2015

2310.   It took six years to make this film.

2311.   The stop-motion animation was so painstaking, the animators could only produce two seconds of footage per day.

2312.   20 animators worked on this film.

2313.   Although there are 17 voice actors, there is no dialogue whatsoever.

2314.   It was released on the Chinese New Year's Day. This is the Year of the Sheep.

2315.   One of the cat's in Animal Control has a mask like Hannibal Lecter.

2316.   The tagline was, "Catch them if ewe can!"

2317.   Shaun's bag has a Blue Peter badge.

2318.   The Farmer's farm is called Mossy Bottom Farm.

2319.   When the Farmer is called Mr. X, he poses exactly like Wolverine from the X-Men series. Wolverine is also known as Weapon X.

A Shaun the Sheep Movie:
Farmageddon
2019

2320. This is the first feature length sequel that Aardman ever made.

2321. The crew studied the film, 2001: A Space Odyssey for certain shots in this film.

2322. The first shot is a parody of the opening shot in the film, Contact.

2323. There is a garage called HG Wheels. This is a reference to the writer, HG Wells. This film parodies War of the Worlds, which was written by Wells.

2324. Rocky from Chicken Run cameos in one shot. He can be seen on a wall holding a coffee mug.

<h2 align="center">Shrek</h2>
2001

2325.   The story is loosely based on William Steig's 30-page book, Shrek! It was released in 1990.

2326.   Nicholas Cage was offered the part of Shrek but he turned it down. Steve Martin, Tom Cruise, Leonardo DiCaprio, and Bill Murray were also considered.

2327.   Chris Farley was cast as Shrek and had recorded 95% of his lines before he suddenly died. He was replaced by Mike Myers.

2328.   Farley's version was extremely different to the finished story since it revolved around a teenage Shrek that didn't want to go into the ogre-business.

2329.   Originally, Mike Myers performed Shrek in a thick Canadian accent. As time went by, he realised that the voice didn't sound right coming out of Shrek's mouth. He insisted that Shrek should have a working-class accent. He demanded to re-record all his dialogue in a Scottish accent.
     There are rumours that this cost the company $4 million dollars but this isn't true. You can hear Myers original voice for Shrek on the DVD extras.

2330.   Janeane Garofalo was cast as Fiona. After Chris Farley died, she was fired. She has no idea why.

2331.   The accent Mike Myers uses for Shrek is how his mother spoke to him as a child when she read him bedtime stories.

2332.   Shrek's appearance was based on a wrestler who suffered gigantism called Maurice "The French Angel" Tillet.

2333.   Shrek is 7ft tall.

2334.   To make Shrek's love scene more convincing, Mike Myers recorded his lines to his wife, Robin Ruzan.

2335.   "Shrek" is Yiddish for "monster."

2336.   Cameron Diaz voices Princess Fiona. She based the character on her sister.

2337.   Robin Williams was supposed to play a role but he had a falling out with the producer.

2338.   In the original story, Shrek was abandoned in a pit by his parents.

2339.   Steven Spielberg nearly made the film in 1991.

2340.   Originally, Donkey looked like Eeyore from Winnie the Pooh.

2341.   Originally, the film was going to splice with live-action like Who Framed Roger Rabbit. The creators also considered making the film with stop-motion.

2342.   Eddie Murphy was nominated for a BAFTA for his role as Donkey.

2343.   The Gingerbread Man is called Gingy. He became the mascot of Wal-Mart soon after the release of this film.

2344.   Shrek's mud shower was so hard to animate, that one of the animators had to take a mud bath to see how the mud moved.

2345.   Shrek has a size 22 shoe.

2346.   In the beginning, Papa Bear, Mama Bear, and Baby Bear can be seen in cages. In a night time scene, Papa Bear is comforting Baby Bear. In a later scene, a rug of Mama Bear can be seen in Farquad's castle.

2347.   The villain, Lord Farquaad, is based on the former Disney CEO, Michael Eisner.

2348.   The Duloc jingle is a parody of Disney's It's A Small World After All. DreamWorks' lawyers were worried that Disney would sue them over the song.

2349.   When Fiona asks Shrek and Donkey about Lord Farquaad, they mock his height. However, when they met Farquaad, there was no way that Shrek and Donkey could see that he was a dwarf.

2350.   Everything in Farquaad's castle is angular. Nothing has curves or bends.

2351.   Farquaad's logo is similar to the Facebook logo.

2352.   As the creators were putting the finishing touches on the film, they realised that they skipped Shrek's line, "What are you doing in my swamp?" The producer had to track down Mike Myers and record him saying this line for the sake of continuity.

2353.   In the 1940 film, Pinocchio, naughty boys are turned into donkeys on Pleasure Island.
        There is an Internet theory that Donkey in this film is one of these boys. This seems possible since Pinocchio exists in this world as well. On top of that, Donkey is one of the only characters that doesn't seem to fit with any other fairy-tale.

Shrek 2
2004

2354.   Princess Fiona has a poster of Sir Justin Timberlake. When the animators came up with this idea, they had no idea that Cameron Diaz was dating Justin Timberlake.

2355.   This is the first animated sequel to be nominated for an Oscar for Best Animated Feature.

2356.   Antonio Banderas voices Puss. He voices the character in the Spanish and Italian dub.

2357.   To help him stay in character, Antonio Banderas wielded a fencing sword while recording his lines.

2358.   Just before Mongo falls into the water, he says, "Be good" to Gingy. This is the last thing ET says in ET: The Extra-Terrestrial.

2359.   Mongo has the same roar as Godzilla.

2360.   In Far, Far Away, there are several parody businesses including Baskin Robin Hood, Farbucks, and Burger Prince.

2361.   The cinema in Far, Far Away is showing a Robin Hood film called Lethal Arrow 4.

2362.   In the original script, the Dragon was going to turn into Pegasus after it drank the potion.

2363.   Shrek's face is made up of 218 muscles.

2364.   Puss in Boots was supposed to have a British accent.

2365.   One of the women who flirts with Shrek says she will "fetch a pail of water." She is later referred to as "Jill."

2366.   This was the most successful film of 2004.

2367.   Jennifer Saunders voices the Fairy Godmother, Dama Fortuna. She was supposed to appear in the previous film.

2368.   When Puss is thrown off Donkey, he screams in Spanish. What he says translates into, "How dare you do this to me, you four-legged bag of meat!"

2369.   There are several hints that imply that King Harold is a frog. In his castle, there is a painting of him standing over a pond.
         Also, his first kiss with the Queen was beside a lily pond.
         When Harold enters the tavern, a female frog looks at him and says, "Do I know you?" Harold is later revealed to be the Frog Prince.

2370.   The writer of the original novel, William Steig, died during production. The film is dedicated to him.

2371.   Dragon and Donkey had six kids called Dronkeys. In future films, there are only five Dronkeys.

2372.   John Cleese and Julie Andrews voice the King and Queen. They recorded their lines together which is very rare for an animated film.

2373.   Larry King voices the Ugly Stepsister. In the British version of the film, Jonathan Ross voices the character.

2374.   A portrait of Elizabeth I can be seen in the castle.

2375.   One of the signs in The Poison Apple bar reads, No one under XXI admitted."

2376.   While Puss is in the pub, he says, "I hate Mondays." This is a reference to feline character, Garfield, who is known for hating Mondays.

2377.   Antonio Banderas had to record the hairball scene for three hours. He damaged his voice during the recording so much, it effected his voice for months.
         Shortly after his recording, he performed the Broadway show, 9. However, the octave range for the musical was lowered because his voice was so strained.

2378.   Originally, King Harold was a nudist.

2379.   When Gingy is watching Knights, the police say that they have spotted Shrek on a "white bronco." This scene is based on the chase in 1994 when police were tracking OJ Simpson who was driving a white Bronco.

2380.   The animators had difficulty making the hair of female characters look realistic. They were struggling so much, a wig weaver visited DreamWorks studio to explain how he makes hair look realistic.

2381.   At one point, the Fairy Godmother says, "What in Grimm's name?" This is a reference to the Brother's Grimm who compiled many classic fairy-tales like Snow White, Cinderella, and Sleeping Beauty.

2382.   Gingy lost his leg in the last film. In this film, he had his limb re-attached with frosting.

2383.   The developers started working on this film before the first film was even finished.

2384.   The entrance to Far Far Away is similar to the entrance of Paramount Studios.

Shrek the Third
2007

2385.   Dragon and Donkey's children are called Bananas, Parfait, Peanut, Debbie, and Coco.

2386.   Julie Andrews voices Queen Lillian. After she knocks down the prison wall, she becomes dazed and sings My Favourite Things and With a Spoonful of Sugar. Both songs were sung by Andrews in The Sound of Music and Mary Poppins respectively.

2387.   The film was shipped to cinemas under the fake title, Stone.

2388.   Amy Poehler voices Snow White.

2389.   Seth Rogen voices the Ship Captain.

2390.   1,373 characters were created for the theatre scene.

2391.   One million man-hours went into making this film.

2392.   The tagline was, "A family movie you will want to see ogre, and ogre, and ogre again."

Shrek Forever After
2010

2393.	Rumpelstiltskin is the villain of this story. He briefly appeared in Shrek the Third but he looked drastically different.

2394.	When Eddie Murphy heard the title, he thought it sounded so bad, he assumed it was a joke.

2395.	One of Rumpelstiltskin's witches is called Baba. She is a witch from Russia mythology called Baba Yaga.

2396.	The story revolves around Shrek and Fiona having marriage problems. To make this look realistic, the studio consulted marriage counsellors for advice.

2397.	Ryan Seacrest voices Father of Butter Pants.

2398.	The original title was Shrek Goes Fourth.

The Simpsons Movie
2007

2399.   The film had 158 drafts.

2400.   The script was so secret that it was shredded after every voicing session.

2401.   Homer calls his pig, Spider-Pig. This is a reference to a character in Marvel Comics called Spider-Ham. His civilian name is Peter Porker.

2402.   Abe has a vision at the beginning of the film. In an earlier script, it was Marge who had the vision.

2403.   20th Century Fox registered the website simpsonsmovie.com in 1997; nine years before the film was green-lit.

2404.   Kevin Bacon had a cameo but his scene was cut.

2405.   The film was sent to cinemas under the codename, Yellow Harvest. This is a reference to Return of the Jedi, which was sent to cinemas under the codename, Blue Harvest.

2406.   Julie Kavner had to do the "Goodbye Homie" scene over a hundred times.

2407.   Edward Norton was supposed to play the man who gets crushed by the dome.

2408.   Only one joke from the first draft made it into the final cut.

2409.   The film cost $75 million. It made $527 million at the box office.

2410.   Albert Brooks plays the villain, Russ Cargill. He is best-known for voicing Marlin in Finding Nemo.

2411.   The villain was supposed to be Hank Scorpio. Scorpio was also voiced by Albert Brooks.

2412.   Moe's Tavern is called Moe's Bar in the film.

2413.   Homer jumps over the gorge at the end of the film. This is an obvious reference to when Homer attempted to jump the gorge in The Simpsons episode, Bart the Daredevil. After Homer fails the jump, he is put into an ambulance. The ambulance immediately crashes into a tree, and Homer falls out and tumbles off the gorge again.

    In this film, you can see the crashed ambulance is still embedded into the tree.

2414.   The film was made by David Silverman. He co-directed Monsters, Inc.

2415.   Halfway through the film, the Simpsons move to Alaska. Weirdly, there is a city in Alaska called Homer.

2416.   When the Simpsons enter Alaska, the border guard gives them $1000. Alaska actually does this but only if the citizen resides there for at least a year.

Sinbad:
Legend of the Seven Seas
2003

2417.   Brad Pitt voices Sinbad. Catherine Zeta-Jones voices Marina. They didn't meet until the film premiered.

2418.   In this story, Sinbad is Greek. In the original story, he is a Muslim from Iraq.

2419.   Russel Crowe was the first choice for Sinbad.

2420.   Michelle Pfeifer voices the villain, Eris. She accepted the role after her children begged her to.

2421.   Sinbad's dog, Spike, was so popular in test-screenings, the filmmakers added in seven more scenes with him.

Sing
2016

2422. The film contains at least 85 songs. Weirdly, three of the songs are by musicians who died in 2016 – Wake Me Up Before You Go-Go by George Michael, Hallelujah by Leonard Cohen, and Under Pressure by David Bowie.

2423. The first scene with Buster Moon was inspired by the opening scene in Jerry Maguire.

2424. When Miss Crawley's eyes pop out, you can see "Made in China" printed on the back.

2425. Miss Crawley is voiced by the director, Garth Jennings.

2426. The film was made by Illumination Entertainment. The company also made The Secret Life of Pets which came out the same year. This is the first time that Illumination released two films in the same year.

2427. Ash the porcupine shoots her quills. Porcupines can't do this in real life. Nor can they talk.

2428. Scarlet Johannsson voices Ash. She provided all her singing.

2429. Seth MacFarlane voices Mike the mouse. Mike is heavily based on Frank Sinatra.

2430. Reese Witherspoon voices Rosita the pig.

2431. Sing is the most successful film in US history that never reached #1 at the box office.

Sleeping Beauty
1959

2432.   In the original German story, Sleeping Beauty is called Briar Rose. In this film (and the Italian version of the story,) she's known as Aurora.

2433.   Aurora's body is based on Audrey Hepburn.

2434.   The original version of Sleeping Beauty is called Sun, Moon, and Talia. It was written by Giambattista Basile. It was published posthumously in 1634. Charles Perrault revised the story in 1697 and it was tweaked again by the Brothers Grimm in 1812.

2435.   Different versions of the story are called The Glass Coffin, Little Briar Rose, and The Young Slave.

2436.   Prince Philip is named after Queen Elizabeth's husband.

2437.   Aurora only has 18 lines.

2438.   Aurora is 16 years old.

2439.   The dance animation used for Princess Aurora and Prince Philip was drawn 25 years earlier for an unfinished short.

2440.   Maleficent's raven is called Diablo. He was supposed to be a falcon.

2441.   It took eight years to make the film.

2442.   Walt Disney wanted the fairies to look identical but the animators refused, saying it was uncreative.

2443.   Real actors were used to carry out the motions of the characters (fighting, dancing, running, etc.) and the animators incorporated the actors' movements to their drawings.

2444.   It took three years to cast Aurora.

2445.   Bill Shirley voices Philip. This was his last acting role.

2446.   When the dragon snaps its jaws, the sound effect is from a castanet.

2447.   Walt Disney was worried that the film was too similar in structure to Snow White and the Seven Dwarfs.

2448.   This was the last fairytale film made by Disney until The Little Mermaid 30 years later.

2449.   Originally, there were going to be seven fairies instead of three.

2450.   The fairies are called Flora, Fauna, and Merryweather.

2451.   Originally, Flora and Fauna were called Tranquillity and Fernadell.

2452.   This is the first Disney animation where the Prince directly defeats the main villain.

2453.   The dragon's movements are based on a rattlesnake preparing to strike.

2454.   The original story has many differences from this film. In the book -
i)   Briar Rose wasn't awakened by true love's kiss. Instead, it said she would wake from her hundred-year slumber with her lover standing before her.
ii)   Briar Rose is guarded by thick thorns instead of a dragon. The dragon was created for the movie to add tension.
iii)   Briar Rose has two children called Dawn and Day
iv)   Briar Rose is a descendant of ogres.

2455.   Aurora is barefoot in every scene except the finale.

2456.   Although there are many versions of Sleeping Beauty, the film is mainly based on the Grimm version.

2457.   Eleanor Audley voices Maleficent. She also voices Lady Tremaine in Cinderella, Betty Rubble in The Flintstones, and Granny in The Looney Tunes cartoons.

2458.   Aurora and Philip dance in the clouds. This shot was nearly used for Snow White and the Seven Dwarfs.

2459.   The clouds above Maleficent's castle are skull-shaped.

2460.   Although it came out in 1959, Sleeping Beauty wasn't released on video until 1986.

2461.   Mary Costa voices Aurora. Walt Disney intentionally never met her until the production ended, worried that her appearance and personality might cause him to alter the character.

2462.   Costa became an incredibly successful singer after the release of this film. She went on to appear in 44 operas and even sang at John F. Kennedy's funeral.

2463.   Maleficent's look is based on Morticia from The Addams' Family. Her head's shape is based on a bat.

2464.   The animation of Maleficent calling upon thunderclouds is taken from the final scene in Fantasia.

2465.   Sleeping Beauty was the most successful film of the year apart from Ben-Hur.

2466.   The film cost $6 million, making it the most expensive Disney animation at the time.
        Although the film made a lot of money, it wasn't considered a success as it cost so much to make. Walt Disney was in so much debt by the time the film premiered, he was forced to slash his animation personnel from 551 to 75 within a year.

Smallfoot
2018

2467.   The story revolves around a group of mythical creatures (yetis) who are terrified of humans. This is the basis for the story of Monsters Inc. and Hotel Transylvania.

2468.   The main male and female characters are Migo and Meechee. These are two different Tibetan words for "yeti."

2469.   The screaming goat is based on the popular YouTube videos of goats unconventionally screaming.

2470.   The yetis hear the humans speak in a high-pitched squeaking sound. These noises were provided by the film's editor.

2471.   In the UK version, Mama Bear is voiced by Spice Girl singer, Emma Bunton.

Smurfs: The Lost Village
2017

2472.   The live-action film, The Smurfs, was released in 2011. The Smurfs 2 was released in 2013. Since they didn't make a lot of money, the studio decided to reboot the franchise as an animated film.

    The only actor who reprised his role from the live-action film is Frank Welker who provides the voice of Gargamel's cat, Azrael.

2473.   Julia Roberts voices SmurfWillow.

2474.   Jonathan Winters provided the voice for Papa Smurf in the live-action films. He was replaced by Mandy Patinkin in this film. The role nearly went to John Goodman.

2475.   The tagline was, "Small is big..." That doesn't even make sense.

2476.   The title was meant to be Get Smurfy.

2477.   The film was delayed by two years.

2478.   Ryan Reynolds was considered for the role of Clumsy.

2479.   Taylor Swift auditioned for Smurfette.

2480.   Mike Myers really wanted to voice Brainy Smurf. When he saw the film, Myers said he hated it.

2481.   This is the first time that Gordon Ramsay played a character in a film that wasn't based on himself.

Snow White and the Seven Dwarfs
1937

2482.   Walt Disney couldn't decide what to make for his first animated feature film – A Princess of Mars or this film. A Princess of Mars was eventually made into the Disney film, John Carter. It is the most unsuccessful film in Disney history and lost nearly $200 million.

2483.   At the time of its release, the plural for dwarf was "dwarfs." When JRR Tolkien published The Lord of the Rings in 1954, his spelling, "dwarves" became the official way to spell it.

2484.   The original title was Seven Little Men Help a Girl.

2485.   Adolf Hitler loved this movie.

2486.   The sound for Dopey's footsteps were created by bending an empty leather wallet.

2487.   In the original story, none of the dwarves are named.

2488.   There was supposed to be a scene where the Evil Queen uses magic to make skeletons dance for her own entertainment.

2489.   At no point in this film does the Evil Queen say, "Mirror mirror on the wall." Instead, she says, "Magic mirror on the wall."
   Weirdly, she doesn't say it in the original story either. Instead, she says, "Magic mirror in my hand, who is the fairest in the land."

2490.   In the Grimm Brothers version of Snow White, the Evil Queen is Snow White's mother. She wanted to eat Snow White's lungs and liver to make herself youthful.

2491.   A scene was cut which shows the dwarves singing about soup.

2492. The Evil Queen's name is Grimhilde.

2493.   25 songs were written for the film. Eight were used.

2494.   The animators didn't like using the word "Dopey" as it sounded too modern in a timeless fairy-tale.

Walt Disney corrected them by saying that the word "dopey" was used in a Shakespeare play. After that, the animators accepted the word "Dopey"… even though it is untrue.

2495.   When Snow White kisses the dwarves goodbye, she doesn't kiss Sleepy.

2496.   Apart from Dopey, none of the dwarves refer to each other by name.

2497.   This was the first animated feature ever made in the United States. Because it had never been done before, many people were certain the movie would fail.

2498.   Although this is often considered to be the first animated film, that honour belongs to El apostol which was made in 1917 by Qurino Cristiani.

2499.   Other names considered for the dwarves were Blabby, Dirty, Gaspy, Busy, Crabby, Wheezy, Thrift, Stubby, Snoopy, Daffy, Flabby, Dumpy, Helpful, Lazy, Scrappy, Sniffy, Gloomy, Hoppy, Jumpy, and Shifty.

2500.   In the original script, the Evil Queen was going to attempt to kill Snow White with a poisoned comb.

2501.   The film was made by 32 animators, 102 assistants, 20 layout artists, 25 background artists, 65 effect animators, 158 inkers, and 167 "in-betweeners."

2502.   The film required two million illustrations and 1,500 shades of paint.

2503.   Sergei Eisenstein said this was "the greatest film ever made." Eisenstien directed the masterpiece, Battleship Potemkin.

2504.   Snow White is the youngest human Disney princess. She is only 14 years old.

2505.   There are only 11 human characters in the film.

2506.   The dwarves names vary in different countries.

2507.   The film had six directors.

2508.   The Prince was supposed to appear throughout the story but his role was shortened as the animators had difficulty drawing him.

2509.   Walt Disney said he would pay any crewmember $5 if they came up with a joke for the film. This inspired the animator, Ward Kimball, to come up with the shot where the dwarves' noses pop up over the bed one by one. Kimball asked Walt for $35.

2510.   Ward Kimball nearly quit the production after two scenes that he animated were cut. Disney made it up to him by letting him animate Jiminy Cricket in Pinocchio.

2511.   Walt Disney attended the premier of this film. He didn't attend another premier until Mary Poppins.

2512.   Walt Disney considered a sequel.

2513.   Dopey was supposed to be voiced by Mel Blanc. Blanc voices Bugs Bunny and is considered to be the best voice actor ever.

2514.   Happy is the only dwarf that Snow White doesn't refer to by name.

2515.   The dwarves say "Jiminy Crickets" at two points in the film. Jiminy Cricket appeared in Pinocchio.

2516.   The film won a special Oscar that consisted of a regular Oscar and seven miniature statuettes.

2517.   The initial budget was $250,000. In the end, the film cost $1.5 million, which was a huge amount for the time. It made over $184 million at the box office, which was four times more than any other film that year. It was the most successful film ever at the time.

Sadly, it only held onto that record for the year when it was eclipsed by Gone with the Wind in 1939.

2518.   Despite the fact that the dwarves mine diamonds every day, there is no explanation with what they do with the diamonds or why the dwarves aren't rich.

2519.   There is an Internet rumour that "Prince Charming" is actually Death and he is taking Snow White to Heaven... that's a bit dark.

2520.   Lucilla La Verne voices the Evil Queen. The first time she performed the Old Witch voice, the animators were astounded by how different she sounded. When they asked her how she did that voice. La Verne said, "Oh, I just took my teeth out."

South Park: Bigger, Longer and Uncut
1997

2521.   The film is R-rated. Paramount asked the writers, Trey Parker and Matt Stone, if they could make the film PG-13. The writers said if they did, it wouldn't be South Park.

2522.   Because the film was Oscar-nominated, Trey Parker and Matt Stone attended the Academy Award ceremony that year. They decided to take acid just before arriving at the ceremony.

2523.   This film marked the first time that Kenny's face is seen.

2524.   The original title was South Park: All Hell Breaks Loose.

2525.   The film was supposed to serve as the finale of the show since the creators were certain it was about to be cancelled.

2526.   It only took a year to make the film.

2527.   Kenny is voiced by Mike Judge, who created the animated series, King of the Hill.

2528.   At the time of its release, this film had the world record for the most offensive words and gestures. The film contains 399 swear words, 199 offensive gestures, and 221 acts of violence. The filmmakers intentionally used 399 swear words knowing that 400 would cause the film to be X-rated instead of R-rated.

2529.   George Clooney voices Dr. Gouache.

2530.   The song, Blame Canada, was nominated for an Oscar. Robin Williams sang it at the award ceremony.

2531.   Brent Spiner voices Conan O' Brien. Spiner is best-known for playing Data in Star Trek.

2532.   In the credits, it says that Saddam Hussein and Satan were played by themselves.

2533.   The tagline was, "Uh-oh."

2534.   Trey Parker said the biggest influence on the story was Victor Hugo's novel, Les Misérables.

2535.   The film cost $21 million. It made $83 million at the box office, making the most successful R-rated animation until the release of Sausage Party.

2536.   Chris Rock said that this is the funniest film he has ever seen.

2537.   There is a poster in the cinema for Mecha Streisand Takes New York.

2538.   When Kenny goes to hell, he is greeted by Hitler, George Burns, and Gandhi.

2539.   The final fight is modelled after the battles in the anime, Dragon Ball Z.

2540.   Heaven has a population of 1,656. Hell has a population of just under a trillion.

Spider-Man: Into the Spider-Verse
2018

2541.   This film was accidentally announced during the 2014 Sony hack.

2542.   The name, Steve Ditko, appears on Jefferson Davis' phone. Steve Ditko created Spider-Man with Stan Lee.

2543.   Olivia is revealed to be Doctor Octopus. This is hinted at since she wears octagonal-shaped glasses and has octagonal lights in her lab.

2544.   Chris Pine provides the voice of Peter Parker, making him the fourth "Chris" to play a Marvel superhero after Chris Hemsworth, Chris Evans, and Chris Pratt.

2545.   Tobey Maguire and John Krasinski were considered for Peter Parker.

2546.   The songs in the Christmas album are Spidey, It's Cold Outside, Swingin' Around the Mistletoe, Silent Night (You're Welcome,) Joy to the World, (That I Just Saved,) Spidey the Snowman, and It's Beginning to Look A Lot Like A Non-Denominational Holiday.

2547.   Krondon provides the voice of Tombstone. This is not the only supervillain he has played. He plays Tobias Whale in the television series, Black Lightning.

2548.   Because the animation style is so surreal, the production had 160 animators.

2549.   The dance that Spider-Man performs in the beginning is a reference to the dance Peter Parker performs in Spider-Man 3.

2550.   The budget was $90 million. It made $375 million at the box office.

2551.   Oscar Isaac cameos as Miguel O' Hara. This is not the first Marvel character that Isaac has played. He played the titular role in X-Men: Apocalypse.

2552.   Many iconic Spider-Man costumes can be seen in Peter Parker's armoury including the Iron Spider, the Stealth Suit, and the suit from the 2018 video game, Spider-Man.

2553.   When Miles gets ready for school, there is a sketch of Leopardon. Leopardon was a robot that Spidey used in the Japanese tv series, Spider-Man. Leopardon also inspired the creation of Mighty Morphin Power Rangers.

2554.   When Miles electrocutes Peter, his nervous system glows for a split-second. When a person is electrocuted in most movies, it is their skeleton that glows, not their nervous system.
         However, nerves conduct more electricity than bones, meaning that this shot is scientifically accurate.

2555.   The film is dedicated to the creators of Spider-Man, Steve Ditko and Stan Lee, who passed away in 2018.

Spies in Disguise
2019

2556.   The tagline is, "Super Spy. Super Fly."

2557.   The trailer came out over a year before the film was released.

2558.   The film stars Ben Mendelsohn, Karen Gillan, Tom Holland, and Will Smith. All of these actors have portrayed superheroes or supervillains. Karen Gillan and Tom Holland worked together in Avengers: Infinity War and Avengers: Endgame.

2559.   This is Will Smith's first animated film since Shark Tale, which came out 15 years earlier.

2560.   The is the second film of 2019 where Tom Holland's character must battle a villain with an army of drones. The other film was Spider-Man: Far From Home. Weirdly, Holland's character goes to Venice in both films.

2561.   The story is based on a 2009 short film, called Pigeon Impossible.

Spirited Away
2001

2562.   This is considered to be the greatest animated film made in Japan. It is also considered to be the best film made by Studio Ghibli or by Hayao Miyazaki. It is the highest rated animated film on IMDb and it is the first anime to receive a score of 100% on Rotten Tomatoes.

2563.   This was the first film directed by Miyazaki where a child character was voiced by a child.

2564.   At one point, Chihiro forcefeeds Haku medicine. To make this look more realistic, the crew recorded a vet feeding a dog and then matched the animal's jaw movements in their animation.

2565.   There are references to the Biblical story, Sodom and Gomorrah, and the Greek myth, Orpheus and Eurydice.

2566.   The witch is called Yubaba. Her name means "Bathhouse Witch."

2567.   The big baby is called Bo. "Bo" is Japanese for "Young Boy."

2568.   In most American animations, the actors record their lines and then the artists animate the characters to match the voices. In this film (and most anime,) it is done the other way around.

2569.   The main character is called Chihiro. Her name means "A Thousand Searches."

2570.   Daveigh Chase voices Chihiro in the English dub. Chase also voice Lilo in Lilo & Stitch.

2571.   Bizarrely, the film didn't have a script. The director showed the whole story to the cast and crew through storyboards. He does this for all his films.

2572.   Haku's name translates into "God of the Swift Amber River."

2573.   While in his dragon form, Haku's movements are based on a gecko and a snake.

2574.   After Chihiro leaves the Spirit World, she loses all memory of her time there.

2575.   Originally No Face had green hair and a very large mouth on his chest.

2576.   The director said the hardest thing about the movie was cutting scenes. If he kept every scene in the finished film, it would've been three hours long.

2577.   Studio Ghibli studied the behaviour of their daughters to make Chihiro's behaviour as accurate as possible. When her parents ask her a question, she doesn't answer until they ask a second time because the crew's daughters were easily distracted.
        Also, when Chihiro puts her shoes on, she taps them into the ground to make them fit properly.

2578.   The executive producer of Pixar, John Lasseter, supervised this film.

2579.   This is the first film ever to earn $200 million before being released in the US.

Spirit:
Stallion of the Cimarron
2002

2580.　The story revolves a wild horse captured by humans. One of the actors is called Mike Horse.

2581.　Spirit was modelled after a three-year-old stallion called Donner.

2582.　It's common practise to have actors imitate animal voices for cats, dogs, horses, etc. for an animated film. To make the film more authentic, real stallions were used for all the horse sounds.

2583.　The clouds in the opening scene are designed to resemble running horses.

2584.　Tom Hanks was considered for the narrator.

The SpongeBob SquarePants Movie
2004

2585.   The film was supposed to be the show's series finale.

2586.   The trailer used footage from the films, Das Boot, The Hunt for Red October, and U-571.

2587.   Scarlet Johansson voices Mindy.

2588.   Alec Baldwin voices Dennis.

2589.   The tagline was "Bigger, squarier, spongier!"

The SpongeBob Movie:
Sponge Out of Water
2015

2590.   Pearl only talks during the credits.

2591.   Although Slash from Guns N' Roses appears in the trailer and a deleted scene, he was absent from the film.

2592.   This film is not be a direct sequel to the last SpongeBob movie. It exists in its own continuity.

2593.   SpongeBob creator, Stephen Hillenburg voices the stroller baby that cries, "SpongeBob!"

2594.   The vortex that Plankton and SpongeBob pass through is based on the wormhole in 2001: A Space Odyssey.

The SpongeBob SquarePants Movie: Sponge on the Run
2020

2595.   The working title was It's A Wonderful Sponge.

2596.   The story is based on the episode, Have You Seen This Snail?

2597.   The film was delayed by a year.

2598.   The previous film inspired a mobile game called Sponge on the Run, which is the title of this film.

Street Fighter II:
The Animated Movie
1994

2599.   When Chun Li reveals data about Shadowlaw, Balrog is referred to as Bison.

2600.   According to the cyborg's database, Chun Li's master is called B. Lee. This is a reference to Bruce Lee.

2601.   The director made a prequel animated series, Street Fighter II: V. It also spawned a prequel film in 1999 called Street Fighter Alpha.

2602.   Steve Blum voices T. Hawk. Although many people may not recognise his name, he is considered to be one of the best voice actors ever and has over 600 acting credits.

2603.   Akuma cameos for a second in the scene where Ryu visits India. Akuma is a secret character in the Street Fighter video game series.

2604.   Bison's terrorist group is called Shadowlaw. In the video games, it's called Shadaloo.

2605.   Many elements from the movie were incorporated into the video game including Bison's scientist, the Shadowlaw jet, Ken's long hair, etc.

2606.   Bryan Cranston voices Fei Long. Cranston is best-known for playing Walter White in Breaking Bad.
    According to the credits, Fei Long is voiced by "Phil Williams" due to voice actor union legalities.

The Sword in the Stone
1963

2607.   Merlin's crankiness and playful manner were based on Walt Disney. Merlin even has the same nose as Walt. Walt didn't know this until the film was released.

2608.   Three actors voice Arthur.

2609.   The short, Winnie the Pooh and a Day for Eeyore, was shown in the cinema before this film.

2610.   This was the first Disney film to be made by a single director.

2611.   Apart from the prologue, Excalibur doesn't appear for 71 minutes. The film is only 79 minutes long.

2612.   The film concludes with a battle between Merlin and Mad Madam Mim. They attack each other by transforming into several different animals.
    Most animators say this scene is one of the most significant scenes in animated history. In fact, many new animators study this scene to see how to animate a creature but maintain its character with easily definable features. Every animal that Merlin turns into looks gentle and every animal that Mim turns into looks evil.

Tangled
2010

2613.   Idina Menzel auditioned for Rapunzel but the producers didn't think her singing was good enough. Shortly after, she was cast as Elsa in Frozen. Kristen Bell also auditioned for Rapunzel. She went on to play Anna in Frozen.

2614.   The original title was Rapunzel. This was changed because Disney execs worried it sounded too "girly" which would stop males from watching the film. They believe this is the reason why Disney's previous film, The Princess and the Frog, didn't make much money.

2615.   Rapunzel's hair weighs 10.4lbs.

2616.   This is the 50th animated Disney film.

2617.   The pub is called The Snuggly Duckling. Originally, it was going to be called The Rotten Corpse.

2618.   14 thugs in The Snuggly Duckling are named – Big Nose, Shorty, Innkeeper, Axel, Bruiser, Attila, Hook Hand, Pirate Thug, Goat Boy, Gunther, Vladimir, Fang, Ulif, Tor, and Killer.

2619.   Walt Disney wanted to make this film in the 1940s.

2620.   In one draft, there was a fortune-telling monkey called Vgore the Visionary.

2621.   In the Brothers Grimm version of this story, Rapunzel's mother steals plants from Gothel's garden. After Gothel catches her, Rapunzel's mother makes it up to her by selling her 12-year-old daughter, Rapunzel.
        Another difference in the Brothers Grimm version is the main male character is the prince and Rapunzel is the peasant.

2622.   Pumbaa and Pinocchio are visible in The Snuggly Duckling.

2623.   Rapunzel's hair is supposed to be 70ft long. It becomes shorter or longer in certain shots to fit on the screen.

2624.   The animators created 100,000 strands of hair for Rapunzel. This is how many hairs a person has on his or her head.

2625.   After Shrek was extremely successful, Disney thought people were getting tired of traditional fairy-tales and thought this film would succeed if it made fun of itself. This argument seemed logical since The Princess and the Frog didn't do well the previous year.
         This version of Tangled was called Rapunzel Unbraided and would have the titular character turn into a squirrel. Thankfully, this idea was scrapped.

2626.   This is the first Disney princess film to be rated PG.

2627.   When Rapunzel is in her crib as a baby, she looks up at a chameleon teddy above her. This teddy is a reference to Pascal, who she meets soon after.

2628.   This film is, by far, the most expensive animated film ever, costing $260 million! It made $592 million at the box office.

2629.   This is longest Disney film since Fantasia.

2630.   Flynn Rider is based on Hugh Jackman, Gene Kelly, Johnny Depp, and David Beckham.

2631.   Rapunzel's parents never speak.

2632.   Originally, Rapunzel was going to use a crossbow.

2633.   Gothel wears a Renaissance dress from the 1780s. This suggests that she was born in this time.

2634.   45,000 lanterns appear in the I See the Light scene.

2635.   Rapunzel is the first Disney princess with supernatural powers.

2636.   Like Frollo in The Hunchback from Notre Dame, Gothel pretends to be a parent to her hostage.

2637. Rapunzel is 18 years old.

2638. Many of the animators have never worked on a film before.

2639. At the end of the film, the king has clearly aged but the queen hasn't. This is because the queen drank the sunflower concoction before she gave birth to Rapunzel.

2640. There are 3,000 people in the Kingdom Dance scene. At the time, this was the most characters to appear in one scene in a Disney film.

2641. Gothel's appearance is based on Cher.

2642. Flynn was going to be called Bastian.

2643. David Schwimmer was cast in a role but his scene was removed.

2644. Ron Perlman voices one of the Stabbington brothers. Jeffrey Tambor voices Big Nose. Both actors starred in Hellboy.

2645. This is the first CGI fairy-tale film by Disney.

2646. Mandy Moore voices Rapunzel. The role nearly went to Natalie Portman or Reese Witherspoon.

2647. Rapunzel's first song was nearly cut from the film.

2648. The film spawned a 2D show called Tangled: The Series in 2017.

2649. Maximus uses a Roman gladius sword. This blade seems fitting since Maximus is a Roman name.

2650. Pascal is a chameleon. He was supposed to be a squirrel.

2651. The Stabbingtons are called Patchy and Not-Patchy.

2652. Pascal was modelled after the producer's chameleon.

2653.   Richard Kiel voices Vlad. Kiel is best-known for playing Jaws in the James Bond series.

2654.   The film spawned a six-minute short in 2012 called Tangled Ever After.

2655.   It's a well-known fact that Rapunzel and Flynn cameo at the beginning of Frozen. Weirdly, the directors of Tangled had no idea that the characters were going to appear in the film until it was released.

2656.   Zachary Levi voices Flynn. He auditioned for the role in a British accent. He uses an American accent for the film.

2657.   The first scene to be completed was the interrogation between Rapunzel and Flynn.

2658.   Rapunzel is always barefoot to represent her innocence. The actress, Mandy Moore, was barefoot while recording her lines.

2659.   The spinning wheel from Sleeping Beauty is in the tower.

2660.   The film was made in two years. By comparison, most Disney films take four years to make. Bizarrely, the last 60% of the animation was completed in the last two months.

2661.   Rapunzel is the first green-eyed Disney princess.

2662.   Gothel only shows her love to Rapunzel's hair, not Rapunzel herself. She only kisses Rapunzel on her hair and strokes her hair when she acts affectionately to Rapunzel. Gothel calls her "my little flower," which is a reference to the sunflower that keeps Gothel young.
         When Flynn shows affection to Rapunzel, he pushes her hair away so he can see her face clearly.

Tarzan
1999

2663.   The story is based on the 1912 book, Tarzan of the Apes, which was written by Edgar Rice Burroughs. Rice went on to write 20 sequels.

2664.   The explorer's camp has a kettle pot that looks like Mrs. Potts from Beauty and the Beast.

2665.   Brian Blessed voices the villain, Clayton. He also performs the famous Tarzan yodel.

2666.   Wayne Knight voices Tantor. Knight voices the main villain in Toy Story 2.

2667.   Clayton was nearly played by Ian McKellen.

2668.   The ship wreck occurs in 1888. The rest of the story takes place in 1911.

2669.   An anatomical professor had to speak with the animators to get an accurate idea of how Tarzan's body should look.

2670.   The story is set in Kenya.

2671.   When baby Tarzan blows bubbles, one of the bubbles is in the shape of Mickey Mouse's head.

2672.   Clayton refers to Zambia at one point even though Zambia didn't exist at the time this film is set in.

2673.   Disney consulted with adoption associations to make Tarzan's revelation more believable when he learns that he was taken away from his family.

2674.   Although Tarzan's movements through the trees is supposed to resemble the movements of a surfer, his animation was created by studying the skateboarding legend, Tony Hawk.

2675.   Lance Henriksen voices Kerchak the gorilla. Harrison Ford was considered for the role.

2676.   In the book, Tarzan's father is killed by Kerchak.

2677.   Rosie O' Donnell voices Terk.

2678.   Tarzan II was released in 2005. It follows Tarzan when he was a child.

2679.   Lemurs appear in the film even though they are only indigenous to the island of Madagascar.

2680.   Tarzan has been adapted more than any story apart from Dracula. This is the 48th adaptation.

2681.   Of all the Tarzan films that exist, this is the only one that is simply called Tarzan.

2682.   Brian Blessed said that Clayton is the best character he has ever played.

2683.   Disney animators looked at a gorilla dissection to understand the animal's muscle structure.

2684.   Some of the filmmakers went to Uganda to watch gorillas in their natural environment. Although they assumed the apes would be ferocious, the crew were surprised how calm and peaceful the gorillas were.

2685.   At one point, a baboon eats a papaya, even though this fruit is indigenous to South America.

2686.   Most of the sounds the gorillas made are from chimps because the gorilla noises sounded too aggressive.

2687.   In the original story, Tarzan was adopted by a fictional ape called a Mangani. This ape resembled a chimp, not a gorilla.

2688.   In the final scene, Tarzan was supposed to go to England as a civilized man.

2689.   Phil Collins performed the movie's song in five different languages.

2690.   Brendan Fraser auditioned for the role of Tarzan. He went on to play a parody of the character in the film, George of the Jungle.

2691.   The film spawned a sequel in 2002 called Tarzan & Jane that takes place a year after the pair get married.

2692.   This is considered to be the last film of the Disney Renaissance.

2693.   Phil Collins won an Oscar for his song, You'll Be in My Heart. Disney didn't win an Oscar for another animated film until 2013 for Frozen.

TMNT
2007

2694.   Leonardo, Raphael, and Donatello have brown eyes. Michelangelo was given blue eyes to make him appear younger and more innocent.

2695.   Some of the monsters are based on mythological beasts including the Yeti, the Cyclops, a gargoyle, and the Jersey Devil.

2696.   Mako voices Splinter. Although he is not well-known in the Western world, he has a cult following and is considered to be one of the most respectable actors in Japanese cinema. He died a year before the film was released. It was publicly announced that Mako would star in the film the day before he died.

2697.   Sarah Michelle Gellar voices April O' Neill.

2698.   Raphael died in the original script.

2699.   Renowned director, Kevin Smith, voices the Diner Cook.

2700.   The Japanese lullaby that Splinter sings was ad-libbed by Mako.

2701.   Chris Evans voices Casey Jones. Chris Evans has played five comic book characters; Casey Jones in this film, the Human Torch in Fantastic Four, Jensen in The Losers, Lucas Lee in Scott Pilgrim vs the World, and Captain America in the Marvel Cinematic Universe.

The Thief and the Cobbler
1993

2702.   This film was in development longer than any movie in history – 28 years.

2703.   Vincent Price voices ZigZag. This was the last film he made as he passed away the same year it was originally released. He recorded his dialogue 20 years before the film was released.

2704.   The film was originally made by Richard Williams. In 1988, Warner Bros took over the production. When Aladdin was released in 1992, Warner Bros. thought The Thief and the Cobbler's story was too similar so the studio abandoned this film.

It was then picked up by a producer called Fred Calvert. Calvert kicked Williams off the project and retitled the film as The Princess and the Cobbler. This version was released in 1993 in Australia and South Africa. This version was considered disastrous and so, was heavily re-edited with new animations and voice actors by Miramax Films.

It was then released in North America under the title, Arabian Knight, in 1995.

2705.   The film cost $28 million. It made a pitiful $319,723 at the box office.

2706.   The uncut version has the most onscreen deaths in movie history – over a thousand.

2707.   Sean Connery was meant to have one line but he didn't show up for the recording.

2708.   The director, Richard Williams, got a bunch of Irish people drunk for the Brigands scene. The actors got so drunk, they ended up fighting each other. The fight was recorded and used for the film.

2709.   Richard Williams was so devastated by the film's failure that he refuses to talk about it. When he attends lectures, he has bodyguards that will remove anyone who mentions The Thief and the Cobbler.

2710.   Williams has never seen the Calvert or Miramax cut. His son watched it and told Williams that "If I ever want to jump off a bridge then I should take a look."

2711.   The film wasn't released in the UK until 2012.

2712.   The director created the animation for the film, Who Framed Roger Rabbit.

The Three Caballeros
1944

2713.   The film revolves around Donald Duck's adventures with a Brazilian parrot called Jose Carioca and a Mexican rooster called Panchito Pistoles. The film was only made to improve the US' relationship with South America during World War II.

2714.   This was the last animated Disney to be released during World War II.

2715.   "Caballero" means "gentleman" in Spanish.

2716.   The film was made alongside the 42-minute animated short, Saludos Amigos. Like The Three Caballeros, Saludos Amigos was only made to improve the relationship between North and South America.

2717.   This is considered to be the most obscure animated Disney film. Many die-hard Disney fans are oblivious to its existence.

2718.   Many people assume Pistoles surname is Spanish for "pistols". However, the Spanish for pistols is "pistolas."

2719.   Although the film never had a sequel, the three main characters appeared in the 1948 film, Melody Time.

Toy Story
1995

2720.   When the director, John Lasseter, showed the script to the producers in 1993, it was a disaster. Woody came across as an arrogant jerk and Buzz Lightyear was annoyingly stupid.

Lasseter was certain that the producers would pull the plug on the whole film. Luckily, he was given another chance.

2721.   Joss Whedon created Rex the Dinosaur.

2722.   The original title was You Are a Toy. The film was nearly called Made in Taiwan and Toyz in the Hood.

2723.   John Ratzenberger voices Hamm. He has appeared in almost every Pixar film.

2724.   Jim Varney voices Slinky. Varney is best-known for playing the titular character in the Ernest series.

2725.   John Morris voices Andy. He voices the character in every movie.

2726.   Magician, Penn Jilette voices the TV announcer on the commercial when Buzz learns he is a toy.

2727.   Mickey Mouse can be seen as one of the clouds in Andy's wall at the start of the film.

2728.   The hardest scene to write was Buzz and Woody's argument at the gas station.

2729.   Buzz's face is based on the director's.

2730.   The film cost $30 million. It made over $373 million at the box office, making it the most successful film of 1995.

2731.   Each of the Army Men have bits of plastic sticking out of their body. This was a problem the toy soldiers had in real life and the animators added it in for authenticity.

2732.   Buzz was supposed to wear a red spacesuit and he was a quarter the size of Woody. His suit was changed to white so it resembled the suits that astronauts wear. Also, his name was going to be Lunar Larry.

2733.   The aliens were voiced by various Pixar crewmembers. They had to suck in helium before recording their lines.

2734.   When Shark wears Woody's hat, he says, "Look, I'm Woody! Howdy howdy howdy!" This is a reference to a Far Side comic strip where a vulture wears a cowboy hat and says, "Hey everyone, look at me, I'm a cowboy! Howdy! Howdy! Howdy!"

2735.   When Woody talks to Slinky on the bed, there is a drawing of Woody in the background. This doodle was an early sketch of Woody.

2736.   Tom Hanks screamed so much as Woody, he suffered chest pains for three days after most recording sessions.

2737.   Woody's meeting before the birthday party required more rewrites than any other scene.

2738.   The Pizza Planet truck in this film appears in almost every Pixar movie.

2739.   When Buzz acts hysterical as Mrs. Nesbit, Woody whacks him with his own dismembered arm.
        The creators took this idea from Arnold Schwarzenegger. When Schwarzenegger was shooting Commando, he wanted a scene where he blows a man's arm off and then beats the man to death with it.
        Although this concept wasn't used for the film, the idea of hitting someone with their own dismembered arm was incorporated into Toy Story.

2740.   The director, John Lasseter wanted Tom Hanks to play the lead role because he believed Hanks is likeable even when he plays a character that is "down-and-out and despicable."
        Lasseter believed the film could only work with Hanks on-board since the audience had to sympathize with Woody even when he acts jealous, petty, and spiteful.

2741.   The Pizza Planet truck gets gas at Dinoco station. Dinoco is the oil company in the film, Cars, which came out 11 years after Toy Story.

2742.   All of Andy's friends have the same body model because Pixar found it too difficult to create different models for children.

2743.   John Lasseter tries to make his films timeless so they will not come across as dated. Because of this, he tried not to have modern toys in the film.

Instead, all the characters had to be toys that have survived at least two generations so they would be universally recognised by children even if kids never played with them.

The only exception to this is Slinky since this toy line ceased in the 1970s.

2744.   The Army Men use a baby monitor so they can speak to Woody. However, the soldiers are using the wrong part of the monitor. The way they have set it up, Woody could speak to the soldiers but not the other way around.

2745.   Woody is seen as an old-school toy who is replaced with revolutionary "cool" toy, Buzz Lightyear. The director based this concept on his childhood experience. As a kid, he loved his Casper doll but threw it away when the new "cool" toy came out; GI Joe.

2746.   Pizza Planet was originally called Pizza Putt and would've been a mini-golf pizzeria. This was changed into a space-themed pizzeria so Buzz would believe he was reaching Star Command.

2747.   Originally, the film was going to revolve a toy called Tinny. Tinny was the main character in 1988 animated short, Tin Toy.

2748.   In Andy's room, there are books on the shelf called Tin Toy, Knick Knack, Red's Dream and Luxo Jr. These are the names of animated shorts made by Pixar in the 1980s.

2749.   The film was nearly a musical.

2750.   Tom Hanks agreed to the role of Woody because he wondered if his toys were alive when he was a kid.

2751.   When Woody dunks his head into a bowl of cereal, no milk spills out because the animators couldn't animate liquid properly at the time.

2752.   Laurie Metcalf voices Andy's Mom. She is best-known for playing Jackie Harris in the TV series, Roseanne, and Mary Cooper in The Big Band Theory.

2753.   The director pitched the film to the studio by saying, "What if your toy was looking for you as hard as you were looking for it?"

2754.   The animators bought tons of toys and took them apart to see how to make them move accurately.

2755.   Bo Peep's appearance in the film references Hans Christian Andersen's fairy tale, The Shepherdess and the Sweep. In this story, toys come to life when children don't look at them.

2756.   Despite the film's legacy, it didn't win a single Oscar apart from an Honorary Award.

Toy Story 2
1999

2757.   Most of the crewmembers worked 36-48 hour shifts during this film. During the making of this film, some of the animators suddenly burst into tears from pure exhaustion.

2758.   The tagline was, "The toys are back in town."

2759.   At one point, Bullseye licks Woody in the face. To make the slurping sound authentic, the animators recorded one of the crew members being licked in the face by a cow.

2760.   Only three animated Disney films have ever won a Golden Globe for Best Picture – this, The Lion King, and Beauty and the Beast.

2761.   Woody's nightmare, the yard sale, and the Buzz Lightyear video game were all supposed to be in the first film.

2762.   The characters in Woody's Roundup look like puppets on strings. In reality, they are computer generated.

2763.   Al never says "Woody" once, even though he's obsessed with him.

2764.   A year after the film's release, an animated series called Buzz Lightyear of Star Command was released.

2765.   At one point, Buzz tells Woody, "You are a toy!" This is a reference to when Woody said this to Buzz in the first film.

2766.   The airport baggage scene was the most complex scene to animate. It took 72 hours to render a single frame during this scene.

2767.   Wayne Knight voices Al. Estelle Harris voices Mrs. Potato Head. Both actors worked on the TV series, Seinfeld.

2768.   John Lasseter voices Blue Rock 'Em Sock 'Em Robot. Lasseter directed Toy Story and Toy Story 2. Lee Unkrich voices Red Rock 'Em Sock 'Em Robot. He directed Toy Story 3.

2769.   Jodi Benson voices Barbie. She voices Ariel in The Little Mermaid.

2770.   This is the first sequel that Tom Hanks ever did.

2771.   The film cost $90 million. It made just under $500 million at the box office.

2772.   When Buzz Lightyear is arrested by the other Buzz, he says, "You are in direct violation of Code 6404.5" This is a law in California that bans smoking in public places.

2773.   In the original script, Bullseye could talk.

2774.   There are many subtle references to the Star Wars franchise (and a few unsubtle ones.)

2775.   Mr. Potato Head stops a door from closing by hurling his hat at it like a Frisbee. He performs the same motion as Oddjob from the film, Goldfinger, when he throws his hat.

2776.   Wheezy is based on Linux's mascot, Tux.

2777.   Jim Varney voices Slinky. He died three months after the film was released.

2778.   When Al hangs up the phone with a Japanese businessman, he says, "Don't touch my moustache." This is a mnemonical joke because "Don't touch my moustache." sounds like the Japanese for "You're welcome."

2779.   90% of the film was deleted by accident! Luckily, the technical director made a copy of the film (without anyone's permission) to show to her kids. When the film was deleted, she had the only copy.
        When it was brought into the office, the animators said that they only lost a week of work. If she didn't make a copy, it's very likely that the film would have never been made.

2780.   The old man that fixes Woody's arm is called Geri. He was in the Pixar short, Geri's Game.

2781.   Jessie tells Woody how she was abandoned in the song, When She Loved Me. Pixar were worried that a three-minute song about love would bore children.

2782.   After Woody has a nightmare, the toys can be seen playing cards. All the cards are the Ace of spades. In fortune telling, this card represents death.

2783.   The canyon that Buzz flies through was created for A Bug's Life but it was never used.

2784.   Over the years, a rumour circulated the Internet suggesting that Jessie's owner is actually Andy's mom. The director confirmed that this is true.

Toy Story 3
2010

2785.   The short, Day & Night, was shown in the cinemas before this film.

2786.   The Western at the beginning was supposed to be in the first film.

2787.   Whoopi Goldberg voices Stretch the octopus.

2788.   The animators said that they watched "pretty much every prison movie" to prepare for the film. The animators found Cool Hand Luke to be the most inspirational movie.

2789.   There are 302 characters in this film.

2790.   The director had his son, Max, draw Daisy's name on Big Baby's pendant.

2791.   Timothy Dalton voices Mr. Pricklepants. He is best-known for playing James Bond.

2792.   At one point, Barbie says, "Authority should derive from the consent of the governed, not from the threat of force!" This is an exact quote from the Declaration of Independence.

2793.   One of Ken's suits is a Nehru, which Blofeld wears in the James Bond film, You Only Live Twice.

2794.   Lotso was originally going to be a Care Bear.

2795.   A lot of babies auditioned for the part of Big Baby. The role went to a baby called Woody.

2796.   The film spawned a series of shorts called Hawaiian Vacation, Small Fry, Partysaurus Rex, Toy Story of Terror, and Toy Story That Time Forgot.

2797.   Jessie and Buzz's dance in the end credits was directed by the choreographers of the show, Dancing with the Stars.

2798.   The Peas-in-a-Pod are based on the Vegimal toy.

2799.   John Lasseter directed the previous two Toy Story films. He let Lee Unkrich direct this film as he wanted to direct Cars 2.

2800.   The film concludes with a shot of clouds that look exactly like Andy's bedroom wallpaper in the first film.

2801.   The villain is a teddy bear. Pixar wanted to make a film with a villainous teddy since 1990.

2802.   This is the only film where Andy says the names of his toys.

2803.   Don Rickles voices Mr. Potato Head. Some reports state that this was the last film he worked on before he died. However, he voiced Frog in Zookeeper which came out a year after this film.

2804.   The film cost $200 million. Toy Story 3 made over a billion dollars at the box office, making it the most successful film of 2010.

2805.   The reason Bo Peep was removed was because the film concludes in an incinerator and she would have melted since she is made of porcelain.

Toy Story 4
2019

2806.   Tom Hanks started recording dialogue for the film in 2015.

2807.   Hanks said that his voiceover work was so intense, it felt like he had performed a four-hour ab workout.

2808.   An action figure of Obi-Wan Kenobi can be seen in the Pinball Machine scene.

2809.   John Lasseter directed Toy Story and Toy Story 2. Although Lasseter was meant to direct this film, he was removed after he acted inappropriately to several writers and so, was replaced with Josh Cooley. This film was Cooley's directorial debut.

2810.   The film was delayed twice.

2811.   This film came out nine years after Toy Story 3, meaning that Toy Story 4 was in production longer than any film in the tetralogy.

2812.   In the closet, Woody talks to a clock called Old Timer. He first appeared in the short, Toy Story of Terror.

2813.   75% of the script was thrown out when two of the writers left in mid-production.

2814.   There are many in-jokes in the antique store.
i)   EVE from Wall-E can be seen in a glass cabinet.
ii)   The Scream cannister from Monsters, Inc is visible in one shot.
iii)   Tinny from the Pixar short, Tin Toy, opens the door for the Pinball Machine.
iv)   Arlo from The Good Dinosaur is on sale in the antique store.

2815.   Duke Caboom was supposed to have a small role but his voice actor, Keanu Reeves, was so entertaining, he was incorporated into the main plot.

2816. The villain, Gabby Gabby, covets Woody's voice box because her one is malfunctioning. Pixar wanted to make a story revolving around this concept since 1988.

2817. Carl Weathers provides the voice of Combat Carl. Weathers is best-known for playing Apollo Creed in Rocky.

2818. When Buzz presses his chest buttons, his voice-box dialogue is mildly distorted compared to the previous films. This is to highlight that his buttons have been overused in the last 20 years, which has damaged his voice-box.
   The reason why Woody's voice-box works even though he is over 50 years old is because it runs on a mini-record, which doesn't sound as clear but it lasts much longer.

2819. Forky was meant to be called Fork Face.

2820. In the first Toy Story, Sid's carpets have the same pattern as the hotel in The Shining. This film also has references to The Shining.
   i)   The ventriloquist dummies' faces were modelled off the bartender, Lloyd.
   ii) The Bear Man cameos in the Lost Toy Bar.
   iii) The typewriter that Woody jumps over in the antique store is the same one that Jack Torrance uses in The Shining.

2821. Bunny was meant to have a cassette player in his tummy.

2822. Although it isn't clear why Forky comes to life, it is believed that it's because Bonnie perceives him as a toy. This makes sense since Hamm is alive because he is perceived as a toy, even though he is a piggy bank.

2823. The tv announcer for the Duke Caboom commercial is Flea from the band, Red Hot Chilli Peppers.

2824. An elderly Mr. Incredible from The Incredibles is sitting at one of the tables in the carnival.

2825. The story takes place two years after Toy Story 3.

2826.   Giggles McDimples is based on the Pinocchio character, Jiminy Cricket.

2827.   The director wrote the story of Inside Out.

2828.   The director and producers performed a blind audio test to cast several actors. When they heard Keanu Reeves' recording for the role, they stopped the audition and immediately cast him.
        They had no idea that the voice they were listening to belonged to Keanu Reeves until the casting director told them.

2829.   When Buzz presses one of his buttons, it says "Open the pod bay doors." This is a line from 2001: A Space Odyssey.

2830.   The keys in the antique store are based on the keys from the Disney game, Kingdom Hearts III.

2831.   The old toys that Bonnie doesn't play with anymore are played by old-time actors, Mel Brooks, Carl Reiner, Betty White, and Carol Burnett. Pixar cast actors who were in their prime in the 70s and 80s to highlight they are "over-the-hill" since Bonnie doesn't play with them anymore.

2832.   Since Annie Potts played Bo Peep in two Toy Story films before, she was aware that a very small amount of what she records will make it into the final film. Since Potts didn't have a complete script, she had absolutely no idea how large her role was until she saw the film.

2833.   Miguel's guitar from Coco can be won as a prize in the same carnival attraction that Bunny and Ducky live in.

2834.   Toy Story 4 came out the same day as Child's Play. By a freakish coincidence, both films revolve around a sentient toy who belonged to a boy called Andy.

2835.   Don Rickles died before he had a chance to reprise his role as Mr. Potato Head. Instead of recasting him the crew looked at all of Rickles material over the years and repurposed some of it as his dialogue for this film.

2836.   The film stars Keanu Reeves, Keegan-Michael Key, and Jordan Peele. All three actors starred in Keanu.

2837.   Many people were upset when the film was announced as fans believed the ending of Toy Story 3 was a perfect conclusion to the trilogy. The writers agreed and said they would never make a sequel unless it was as good as Toy Story 3.

2838.   Duke Caboom first appeared in Incredibles 2 as one of Jack-Jack's toys.

2839.   When Woody reunites with Bo, her sheep bring a Grape Soda cap. This is the same cap that Ellie pinned on Carl's shirt in Up.

2840.   When Duke Caboom is talking about himself, the Canadian National Anthem can be heard in the background.

2841.   Like his character, Keanu Reeves rides a motorcycle and has his own company that designs custom motorcycles.

2842.   Gabby Gabby is a reference to the 1960s doll, Chatty Cathy. She is also based on Talking Tina from The Twilight Zone episode, Living Doll.

2843.   The last thing Keanu Reeve's character says is, "Whoa." This is a reference to Reeves' character, Ted in the film, Bill & Ted's Excellent Adventure. In that film, Ted regularly says "Whoa" anytime he sees something cool.

Transformers: The Movie
1986

2844.   This film is set in 2005; 20 years after the second season of the animated series, Transformers.

2845.   John Moschitta Jr. voices the super-fast talking Blurr. Moschitta was in the Guinness Book of World Records for being the world's fastest talker.

2846.   The film had a surprisingly good cast including Leonard Nimoy, Eric Idle, Judd Nelson, Casey Kasem, and Orson Welles.

2847.   In some countries, the film is called Transformers Apocalypse! Matrix Forever!

2848.   Frank Welker voices Megatron. Although many people have never heard of the actor, he is considered to be the greatest voice actor of modern times. He has over 800 acting credits to his name.

2849.   The Transformers toy line was created by Hasbro. They killed off 14 Transformers in this film and replaced them with new characters so they could bring out new toys.

2850.   Orson Welles voices the villain, Unicron. When Welles was asked what the film was about, he said, "I play a big toy who attacks a bunch of smaller toys."

2851.   When Unicron roars, the sound is from the Hulk in the 1982 cartoon series.

2852.   Unicron was originally going to be called Ingestor.

2853.   The script was written in one day.

2854.   In the original script, the Transformers' home planet, Cybertron, was going to turn into a robot and fight Unicron.

2855.   According to the credits, the songs, Nothin's Gonna Stand in Our Way and Hunger, were performed by Spectre General. This isn't true. The songs were performed by Kick Axe. The director changed their name in the credits because he thought "Kick Axe" sounded too threatening. The band didn't know about this change until the film was released.

2856.   The tagline was, "Beyond good. Beyond evil. Beyond your wildest imagination."

2857.   The film cost $6 million. It only made $5.85 million at the box office.

2858.   Arcee's head is styled like Princess Leia's hair from Star Wars.

2859.   This was the last film Orson Welles ever made. Welles was so ill when he did his voiceover work, that some have suggested Leonard Nimoy voiced some of Welles' scenes. This is not true.

Treasure Planet
2002

2860.   This film took ten years to make.

2861.   The lead, Jim Hawkins, was based on James Dean.

2862.   Joseph Gordon-Levitt voices Jim Pleidas Hawkins. Pleiadas in the Taurus constellation. This is a reference to Jim's obsession with astronomy.

2863.   Emma Thompson voices Captain Amelia.

2864.   Treasure Planet cost $140 million. Sadly, this film made less than $110 million at the box office. Because Disney spent $40 million on advertising Treasure Planet, the film lost a total of $79 million. This means the film lost more money than any other Disney animation.

2865.   The look of the film was based on an oil painting.

2866.   This is Disney's third adaption of the story, Treasure Island. Disney released Treasure Island in 1950 and Muppet Treasure island in 1996.

2867.   Jim's clothes get lighter in colour as the story progresses.

Trolls
2016

2868.   The film is based on the Trolls toyline which was created by Thomas Dam in Denmark in 1958.

2869.   John Cleese voices King Gristle. This is the second time he has voiced a king in an animated film. He voices King Harold in Shrek 2.

2870.   The original toys were filled with wood shavings.

2871.   Gwen Stefani voices DJ Suki.

2872.   The line, "He who controls the trolls controls the kingdom" was inspired by the quote in Frank Herbert's Dune, "Whoever controls the spice controls the universe."

2873.   This is DreamWorks first animated musical since The Road to El Dorado.

2874.   Russel Brand voices Creek.

Trolls World Tour
2009

2875.   The concept of gathering six strings together is a parody of the storyline of Avengers: Infinity War.

2876.   The film is directed by David Smith. This is his directorial debut.

2877.   This is the first Universal animated film to be released in April.

2878.   The creators of the film realised they couldn't call it "Trolls 2" as it's too similar to Troll 2, which is often considered to be the worst film ever made.

Up
2009

2879.   The short, Partly Cloudy was shown in the cinema before this film.

2880.   It took five years to make this film.

2881.   All the good characters are shaped with circles and rectangles. All the villains have triangular shapes on their face (pointy ears, noses, mouth, etc.)

2882.   This is the first Disney film to reference infertility or divorce.

2883.   This was the first film nominated for an Oscar for Best Picture and Best Animated Feature.

2884.   Carl's face is based on Spencer Tracey. His voice is based on Walter Matthau.

2885.   The dogs literally take part in a dogfight (airplane battle) at the end.

2886.   The film's codename was Helium.

2887.   Jordan Nagai voices Russell. This was his film debut.

2888.   Muntz has the same sword that William Wallace had in the film, Braveheart.

2889.   The villain, Charles Muntz, is named after Charlie Mintz; the man who stole Walt Disney's first creation, Oswald the Lucky Rabbit. Disney countered this by creating Mickey Mouse.

2890.   The director voices Kevin the bird.

2891.   Alpha forces Dug to wear the Cone of Shame to humiliate him. A Florida science teacher called Laurie Bailey-Cutkomp thought this was such a good idea, she forced her students to wear a Cone of Shame if they spoke out of turn.

Surprisingly, the teacher wasn't fired because "finding licensed science teachers in America is really hard."

2892.   Carl and Ellie have a picnic under the tree from the film, A Bug's Life.

2893.   When Carl and Ellie are kids, only Ellie speaks. When they are adults, only Carl speaks.

2894.   In the German dub, the dogs are distracted by a cat, not a squirrel.

2895.   In the original story, Kevin laid eggs that could reverse aging. This was the reason Charles Muntz desired the bird so much. This concept was removed for being "too bizarre."

2896.   Kevin is named after Kevin Spacey.

2897.   A rip-off of the film called What's Up: Balloon to the Rescue was released the same year.

2898.   When Charles Muntz speaks on a podium in the beginning scene, the animators didn't create an audience. Muntz is literally talking to a bunch of hats. The animators did this to save time.

2899.   The French short film, Above Then Beyond, revolves around an old woman who turns her house into a hot air balloon to avoid eviction. Since this short was released three years before Up, some people believe that this film is a rip-off of Above Then Beyond. However, this is impossible since Up began production one year before Above Then Beyond was released.

2900.   20,622 balloons are used to lift Carl's house. It would take 12,658,392 balloons to lift Carl's house in real life.

2901.   Elie Docter voices Ellie. She is the director's daughter.

2902.   Christopher Plummer voices Muntz.

2903.   Carl is 78 years old.

2904.   The DVD includes the short, Dug's Special Mission.

2905.   The film cost $175 million. It made $735 million at the box office.

2906.   The intro is considered to be the saddest movement in Pixar history. Even when the filmmakers were looking at the storyboard, some crewmembers started crying.

2907.   The film won an Oscar for Best Original Score and Best Animated Feature.

Wallace and Gromit: Curse of the Were-Rabbit
2005

2908.   The film needed 2.8 tons of Plasticine to make all the character models.

2909.   A thousand baby-wipes were needed every week to wipe the Plasticine off the animators' fingers.

2910.   Two stop-motion films were released in 2005 – this film and Corpse Bride. Helena Bonham Carter starred in both.

2911.   Straight after the film was released, the animators warehouse burned down, destroying all the character models.

2912.   The animators managed three seconds of footage per day.

2913.   The Were-Rabbit attacks a shop called Harvey's. This is a reference to the film, Harvey, which is about a man who is friends with a gigantic rabbit.

2914.   Wallace regularly mentions how much he loves cheese. Cheese sales skyrocketed during the release of this film.

2915.   Vegetable themed posters can be seen in the town like Carrot on a Hot Tin Roof and Spartichoke.

2916.   Wallace is based on the director's father.

2917.   The tagline is, "Something wicked this way hops."

2918.   The film won an Oscar for Best Animated Feature.

2919.   44lbs of glue had to be used every month to keep the sets stuck down.

2920.   43 versions of Gromit and 35 versions of Wallace had to be created for the film.

2921.   Comedian, Peter Kay, voices PC Mackintosh.

2922.   Lady Tottington's design changed 40 times.

2923.   The water was created with CGI, not stop-motion.

2924.   Peter Sallis voices Wallace. He has voiced the character since his first appearance in the 1989 short, A Grand Day Out. DreamWorks wanted Wallace to be voiced by a famous actor that American audiences would recognise. The company refused, believing that nobody could voice Wallace apart from Sallis.

2925.   New eyes had to be made for each character every two months.

2926.   The Were-Rabbit model broke three times in the final scene.

2927.   The directors jokingly call The Curse of the Were-Rabbit "the world's first vegetarian horror film."

2928.   Ray Harryhausen visited the set. He is the greatest stop-motion director of all time.

WALL-E
2008

2929.   The short, Presto, was shown in the cinemas before this film.

2930.   The film's working title was Trash Planet.

2931.   Ben Burtt voices 80% of the cast including the titular character. He personally recorded 2,500 sound effects for the film.

2932.   EVE solves a Rubik's Cube in four seconds. The world record is 5.5 seconds.

2933.   AUTO was inspired by HAL 9000 from 2001: A Space Odyssey. WALL-E's pet cockroach is also called Hal.

2934.   Crush and Squirt from Finding Nemo appear in the credits.

2935.   WALL-E and EVE don't speak to each other for 22 minutes.

2936.   The original plot involved green aliens kidnapping EVE.

2937.   The writers considered making the humans speak a new language.

2938.   WALL-E only says EVE's name correctly twice.

2939.   The sound of EVE's laser blasts was partly created by tapping a slinky.

2940.   This story takes place in 2805 AD.

2941.   Sigourney Weaver voices the Ship's Computer. This is the third time she has voiced a spaceship computer. She voiced the ship in the animated series, Futurama, and the film, Galaxy Quest.

This is also the second time she has worked on a Pixar film. She voices the intercom at the Marine Life Institute in Finding Dory.

2942.   AUTO is not voiced by an actor. His voice was created as a text-to-speech program for the 1984 Apple Macintosh.

2943.   The last piece of space junk visible as WALL-E leave's Earth's orbit is the first satellite in space, Sputnik 1.

2944.   To make the ruined world look realistic, the art director studied images of Chernobyl.

2945.   WALL-E stands for "Waste Allocation Load Lifter - Earthclass."

2946.   EVE stands for "Extra-terrestrial Vegetation Evaluator."

2947.   The ship is called the Axiom. An axiom is a part of math that is absolute or taken for granted.

2948.   The sound for the insect clicking was from locking handcuffs.

2949.   The sound for the cockroach chirps were from raccoons on fast-forward.

2950.   The wind sound was created by dragging a bag along a carpet.

2951.   The Axiom's paths are color-coded; the blue ones are for humans, the white ones are for robots, and the red ones are for stewards.

2952.   The tagline was, "In Space, No One Can Hear You Clean."

2953.   One of the programmers, Justin Wright, died of a heart attack while working on the film. He was only 27 years old. The film is dedicated to him.

2954.   Most Pixar films require 75,000 storyboards. This film needed 125,000.

2955.   The person who designed EVE also designed the iPhone and the iPod.

2956.   Twinkies and cockroaches can be seen throughout the film. This is a reference to the myth that Twinkies and cockroaches can survive any apocalyptic scenario.

2957.   The DVD has a short called BURN-E that shows the adventures of a robot on the Axiom.

2958.   WALL-E makes skyscrapers out of trash. It takes approximately 95 years for him to build one of these skyscrapers.

2959.   The Pixar team had to watch every Charlie Chaplin and Buster Keaton film every day during lunch for 18 months. This was to help them tell a story without dialogue.

2960.   WALL-E's name is a reference to Walt Disney. His full name is Walter Elias Disney.

Wreck-It Ralph
2012

2961. The short, Paperman, was shown in the cinema before this film.

2962. The studio said that Nintendo was very particular about how their characters were portrayed. During the Bad Guy meeting, one Nintendo executive said, "Bowser would NEVER hold a tea cup like that!"

2963. Zangief from the Street Fighter series attends the Bad Guy meeting, even though he is a hero in the video game.

2964. This is the first Disney film to show gun violence since Atlantis: The Lost Empire.

2965. Kano from Mortal Kombat performs his finishing move during the Bad Guy meeting.

2966. Due to copyright reasons, Kano was renamed as Cyborg.

2967. Originally, most of the characters (including Ralph) were going to look 8-bit.

2968. Peach and Daisy from the Mario series can be seen in Central Midway.

2969. The four main characters don't meet for 82 minutes.

2970. A piece of graffiti that reads, "Leerooooy" can be seen on the right side of the tunnel. This is a reference to Leeroy Jenkins who gained Internet fame playing the video game, World of Warcraft.

2971. King Candy's voice is based on Ed Wynn. Wynn voices the Mad Hatter in Alice in Wonderland. Alan Tudyk won the role of Candy after doing a perfect impression of Wynn during his audition.

2972. When Fix-It-Felix jumps, he makes the same sound as Mario when he jumps in Super Mario RPG.

2973.   The film was nearly made in the 1980s.

2974.   The developers were trying to find a way to incorporate Mario into the story. After a while, they gave up because they didn't want to put him in the film just for the sake of it.

2975.   The guns from Hero's Duty make the same sound effect as the lasers in Terminator 2: Judgement Day.

2976.   Originally, the film was going to be called High Score.

2977.   The tagline is, "The story of a regular guy just looking for a little wreck-ognition."

2978.   The film was released on the 75-year anniversary of Walt Disney's first animated film.

2979.   The bartender is from the 1983 game, Tapper.

2980.   King Candy's safe is locked with a NES controller.

2981.   King Candy's password is Up, Up, Down, Down, Left, Right, Left, Right, B, A, Start. This is one of the most famous cheats in video game history. It was a cheat in the Konami game, Contra.

Zootopia
2016

2982.   The film is called Zootropolis in Europe.

2983.   Originally, the film was supposed to revolve around Nick Wilde. However, test audiences had difficulty relating to the character so Judy Hopps was made the lead character.

2984.   There are no reptiles, birds, fish, or amphibians in the movie.

2985.   Idris Elba voices Bogo. Bogo's name is derived from the Swahili word "mbogo," which means "buffalo."

2986.   Judy was given purple eyes because the animators thought her grey fur made her look boring.

2987.   The film cost $150 million. This is the second animated Disney film to gross a billion dollars.

2988.   The film is 108 minutes long, making it the longest animated Disney film apart from Fantasia.

2989.   The pirated DVDs at Duke Weaselton are parodies of Disney films including Meowana (Moana,) Wrangled (Tangled,) and Pig Hero 6 (Big Hero 6.)

2990.   Alan Tudyk voices a weasel called Duke Weaselton. In Frozen, he voices the Duke of Wesselton (which is incorrectly called Weaseltown.)

2991.   Clawhauser is based on Jerry from the comedy, Parks and Recreation.

2992.   Shakira voices Gazelle.

2993.   There are many sight gags including the cereal, Lucky Chomps (Lucky Charms,) Lemming Bros. Bank (Lehman Bros.,) Zoogle (Google,) Pawpsicle (Popsicle,) and MuzzelTime (FaceTime.)

2994.   Every sheep has rectangular pupils except Bellwether.

2995.   Wolford is a wolf that patrols undercover as a ram. This is a reference to the phrase, "Wolf in sheep's clothing."

2996.   Woolter and Jesse are parodies of Walter and Jesse from the tv series, Breaking Bad.

2997.   Several musicians can be seen on Judy's music player. All their names are animal-based puns e.g. The Beagles, Gun N' Rodents, Kanine West, Mick Jaguar, Hyena Gomez, The Fur Fighter, Catty Perry, Destiny's Cub, and Ewe 2.

2998.   Nick Wilde's design is based on the titular character from the 1973 film, Robin Hood.

2999.   Disney animators have to work gruelling hours, which leaves them exhausted. They believe staying caffeinated is so important for their job, the man who supplies coffee for the animators, Carlos Benavides, is credited for this film. His job title in the credits is Caffeination.

3000.   Aladdin's magical lamp is on Yax's shelves.

www.ingramcontent.com/pod-product-compliance
Lightning Source LLC
Chambersburg PA
CBHW071406090426
42737CB00011B/1369